# CHELMSFORD

## A Stroll Through Time

Peter A.T. Turrall M.B.E.

1888 - 1975          1975 onwards

Coat of Arms of Chelmsford

First Published in 2002 by Peter Turrall

ISBN 0-9542055-0-2

Printed in Singapore by Craft Print International Ltd

# Preface

The inspiration to write this book came about through a conversation at my house on Sunday 24th March 1996 with Mrs. Con Johnson, ex Mayor of Chelmsford, a music lover, member of many local organisations and secretary of the Friends of Chelmsford Museum.

As a collector of old Chelmsford postcards which I catalogue into various parts of the town, Mrs. Johnson was keenly interested in seeing them as one of her organisations was due to put on a public showing of cards and memorabilia depicting "Vanishing Chelmsford".

Mrs. Johnson, or "Con" as she prefers to be known, immediately decided that my collection should be used as part of the public presentation, and so the start of my book was inspired by Con's persuasive powers. She is a wonderful, dedicated and knowledgeable person who only came to live in this town when her husband a Sales Director started work at a local company in 1965.

Con immediately fell in love with Chelmsford and, since her arrival, she has engaged herself in spreading the gospel on the attributes of this, the County Town of Essex. For one who originated in the Malvern Hills, she is an inspiration to all Chelmsford citizens and it was no surprise when, as a Borough Councillor, she was elected to the High Office as Mayor of Chelmsford in 1984.

I have worked alongside Con in a number of ways particularly in charity work. She breeds ideas which are always good. Her inspiration is unmatched and because of this I dedicate my book to her, my wife Jean, who is a member of the well known Pennack family of undertakers, my children Howard and Carolyn, and my little grandsons Thomas and Edward on whom it will fall to continue this part of the Turrall family.

Peter A.T. Turrall M.B.E.
October 2001

# Acknowledgements

My thanks are due to:-

Mrs. Con Johnson M.A. (Hon) for the inspiration she gave and the encouragement to write this book.

My wife Jean for putting up with the long hours I spent compiling this book in my computer room.

My daughter Carolyn for continually persisting that I publish this book. My son Howard for his comments and additives to some of the chapters.

Claire Lucas an ex-colleague when I was employed as Publicity and PR Manager at GEC-Marconi Communications in Chelmsford for all her work in typing the drafts and scanning in all photographs and proof reading.

To those people whose photographs I have used in this book. They are from my own collection of postcards put together over many years.

To Colin Pooley, friend for many years and Publishing Consultant, for all his helpful advice and patience in ensuring this book was printed in accordance with current requirements.

To Fred Spalding (deceased) who through his expert photographic work over many years in recording every aspect of Chelmsford life has preserved forever a wonderful record of scenes, people and events in this, our county town - some of which are included in this book.

To people not mentioned by name who in some way have helped me with information or practical help in getting this book published and printed.

# Contents

# Chapter One

# INTRODUCTION

Chelmsford is my birthplace. I was born to Arthur and Blanche Turrall at Number 30, Hill Road. My father, one of seven brothers, worked in the Licensing Department of the Essex County Council at County Hall in King Edward Avenue and was a very keen sportsman. He was born near Brentwood, brought up in Kelvedon and then came to Chelmsford in the early 1920's. My mother, also one of seven, was born in the heart of Chelmsford in Fairfield Road opposite where the Civic Theatre is situated now. My younger brother Michael was also born in Hill Road and, together with my mother, we consider ourselves true Chelmsfordians.

After five years in Hill Road, my father and mother moved to the other side of Chelmsford where they purchased a new property in Widford. My early education was at the Trinity Road School where I was taken by my Governor, one Daisy Rolph who lived in Navigation Road. I then went to the old Widford School for two years before entering the brand new Moulsham School, now known as Moulsham High School. Later I went to the Technical School as a part-time student (the war was still on) in Market Road and completed my higher education at the Dovedale Centre in Moulsham Street.

My real awareness of my birthplace town began when I joined the staff of Chelmsford Borough Council in 1946 in the building known as Rainsford House. This was situated on the site where the Civic Centre now stands in Duke Street.

I was employed as a Junior Clerk. The war had just ended but conscription was in force and the Senior Clerk above me was just about to join the RAF as I came on the scene. The job description was really misleading as I was a glorified errand boy, telephone operator, tea maker and a fetcher of the buttered buns and buttered rolls from Mr. Newcombe's Café across the way near where later one of Chelmsford's night clubs used to stand.

In those days the Chelmsford Town Council consisted of a large number of Aldermen and Councillors plus the Council Chief Officials. My immediate bosses were called Committee Clerks. I remember their names as Eke, Walker and Holwill, all members of the Town Clerks Department. They took minutes of Council meetings, the typists put them in to readable form and then they had to be printed.

Sounds simple enough but somebody - me - had to take the typed efforts to the printers, Messrs. Duttons in Tindal Street, not just once but sometimes several times a day and bring back for checking those which had already been set.

What I did not know was that the agenda for the Council meeting had to be delivered by hand to these forty Aldermen, Councillors and Chief Officials, not on working days, but on Saturdays. Furthermore their houses were scattered all over the Chelmsford area and I was expected to take the agenda one Saturday and the heavy Council minutes the following Saturday to all these people on my bicycle. No bag was provided for the bulk of paper and no extra money for working on a Saturday and certainly no waterproofs for the often inclement weather.

When I asked for money to repair a puncture, I got a very stern look from the Town Clerk George Barford and his Deputy Victor Sharman. Incidentally, I even had to deliver the Town Clerk's minutes to his house whilst he was playing golf on a Saturday morning.

Having outlined the above, I come to the point of getting to know Chelmsford. Fortunately I have a photographic memory and therefore names and addresses were no problem. Travelling around Chelmsford - I covered just over 25 miles delivering Council papers - I became aware of buildings and people. This has enabled me to write this book with some authority. My recollections are not meant to be precise - they are a reminder of past happenings, buildings and people.

I have travelled widely in the Chelmsford area and met many people. Having left the Borough Council job to serve my National Service, I decided not to go back when this was complete as it meant I would once again be tied to Saturday afternoons which would interrupt my football and cricket. I therefore took a job in Industry with the Marconi Wireless and Telegraph Company rising to the position of Director of Exports before settling down to a home based position as Publicity Manager. I therefore have a wide knowledge of industry in the town, particularly that of Marconi.

No research has been made in the preparation of this book. It is purely from memory over fifty years. Names are real and events as recorded happened. No offence is meant in mentioning people's activities or actions or the omission of names of some people, shops or buildings. In other words I have highlighted only those which either had some influence on my early life or those in which I had contact.

# Chapter Two

# THE HIGH STREET

The centre of Chelmsford has to be the place where this book starts. The High Street has changed its character over many years. Officially it starts from the Shire Hall at the top end and finishes near the Stone Bridge at the bottom.

For many years, even after the arrival of motorised transport, the High Street carried two-way traffic from the Moulsham end and from the Duke Street end. Halfway up the High Street traffic could turn into London Road and a little further on into Springfield Road.

Let us start at the top end and work our way down recording shops, events and characters. As will be noted in a later chapter, the Shire Hall looks down on the High Street where, in front, stood the Sebastapol Cannon, now relegated to Oaklands Park in Moulsham Street where the Chelmsford and Essex Museum is situated.

As a young boy I spent many happy moments trying to sit astride this Cannon whilst my mother did her shopping in the town.

The old Post Office with its Victorian style counters stood at one side of the Shire Hall adjacent to Barclay's Bank. Next door was the Saracen's Head Hotel. Many famous people have stayed here either overnight or fairly long term. One such visitor at the turn of the century was Signor Guglielmo Marconi whilst visiting his factory a little way down the road in New Street. Just a little way along was the Tindal Cafe, a place where many of the bank employees and those of other offices nipped out for their morning coffee and lunch time breaks.

Further along was Spalding's. The main shop sold up-market toys and most little boys and girls pressed their noses against the glass windows admiring these wonderful items.

Alongside Spalding's, now the site of the National Westminster Bank, was a little area called Crane Court. It was along here that Mr. Fred Spalding had access to his photographic studio. Mr. Spalding is well known for the wonderful photographs of Chelmsford and its surrounds. We owe a lot to this man with such great foresight and his postcards are collectors' items. Many in this book are those which I have managed to purchase over the years.

Also in Crane Court was the access to a number of other places including the Madie Russell Dance School. This was a very famous school where all budding dancers from the town sought the guidance of the tutor. The Essex County Cricket Club had its headquarters here as well as Cecil Bocking the Chiropodist, the Chelmsford Boys' Club and the office of NALGO (National Association of Local Government Officers).

Continuing down on the same side of High Street, I remember the small Westminster Bank. On many occasions I had to take the cash from Jefferys the Outfitters, near the Stone Bridge, where I had a Saturday morning job as my Uncle, Lionel Hills, was the manager there.

The Freeman, Hardy and Willis shoe shop came next followed by Rippon's, then Self and Hicks who sold babies' wear. Parkes the Chemists shop, Perkins the hairdressers and then Chapman the Jeweller run by Mr. Raven who, if I remember correctly, was a leading member of the Chelmsford Rotary Club.

A bit further down was Joseph Gripper the ironmongers. If you wanted anything to do with tools, screws, nails or anything else in that line, you either went to Gripper's or Hasler and Hance in the Back Street. Next door was the passageway to the rear of many shops including access to Cramphorns Corn and Seed Merchants who had their shop on the other side of this passage. There you could go and buy loose corn for your hens, seeds for your budgerigar, parrot food and anything connected with home produce, including flower and vegetable seeds. All the men working in the shop wore khaki coats.

Nearby was the Scotch Wool and Hosiery Store, Luckin Smith's grocers shop, the Co-op Furniture shop whose manager was a Mr. Skilton - Peark's Dairies, the Chelmsford Conservative Association Headquarters, Joy's the Ladies costumiers and then Fletcher's the Butchers. A little further on was the office of what was called the Weekly News, one of the up-market local papers. Many times I had to take official notices from the Borough Council to this office where they were received by the Chief Clerk Mr. Woolford whose daughter Iris is a well known Chelmsford personality, particularly at the Cathedral.

Adjacent to the Weekly News, now the property of the Royal Bank of Scotland, was a surgery accessed at the side to the upstairs room where Dr. Pitts held council over his patients.

Next door was Bond's the large department store, now operating under the name of Debenham. A rather expensive place to shop but it was frequently visited by the upper echelon of the day.

Marks and Spencers were on the other side of Bond's. This was a much smaller store than the one which stands opposite today. The Manageress was a well endowed lady by the name of Mrs. Vera Wyatt. Her very appearance made one tremble but beneath this exterior she was a very kind lady who later, with her husband Maurice, opened a corner shop in Wood Street at the other end of the town.

Easiphit Shoe Shop was next to Marks and Spencers followed by the Dane Dye works where people had their suits and other clothes cleaned on the premises. Macfisheries came next and it was here that I queued on many a day to get a very good pint of Harwich shrimps for my parents. They also did a good line in bloaters and kippers, all on a wet slab, something which would not be permitted these days. The highlight of this shop was the imitation seal in a tank of bubbling water in the middle of the fish slab.

Right on the corner of Springfield Road was Boots the Chemist. This was the place where most people came to collect their requirements of pills and plasters, I remember the manager was a Mr. Bradnam, who it was alleged, was related to Donald Bradman the famous Australian cricketer, but changed the spelling of his name as he was fed up being the lesser of the two Bradmans.

We move across Springfield Road where the Fifty Shilling Tailors stood. I remember my parents bought my first suit here for £2 when I was about to start my duties in the Town Clerk's Office. Woolworths was the next shop. Always known as the 3d and 6d store, it was the delight of every young boy and girl to spend their limited pocket money in this place. At some time either during or just after the war, a fire took place in the store and they had a sale of damaged items. Being one of the early persons on the

scene, I managed to buy some super pens, notebooks and drawing instruments.

Where the Meadows entrance now stands was a wonderful grocery store called Liptons. The manager was a short plump gentleman with dark wavy hair who was very kind and on many occasions gave me an extra item although rationing was still in operation. I think his name was Mr. Sexton.

Banham's the butchers was the next shop, who were regarded as one of the best butchers in the town. A Mr. Barnard worked there. He obviously was a friend of my Aunt Doris as many a time I was asked to go and see him for the odd "tit bit". A number of Banhams worked in the shop and the cash desk was occupied by one of their wives.

Williamson's café was adjacent. This was the up-market gathering place for the daily shoppers where black-dressed waitresses with white aprons and little white caps served tea and coffee. Part of my Saturday job was to go and collect coffee and "wads" for the staff of Jeffreys and later return the silver tray and coffee pots to this place. Norman Stanley the Wireless shop stood next to Williamson's. Many Chelmsford people bought their first wireless set from this shop.

Adjacent stood the now demolished Methodist Church. The tall Cater building now stands on this site. My only recollections of this Church is the wedding of a certain Mr. Lovegrove and his bride where my younger brother Michael sang a solo called "I'll Walk Beside You".

Now we cross over the road and right against the Stone Bridge was a ladies' dress shop called Williams. The manager was a Mr. Lamb - you can imagine what his nickname was. I often had a quiet laugh as he was a rather prim and proper character.

My Uncle Lionel Hills was the manager of the next shop called Jeffreys, a gentlemens' outfitters. Lionel was called into the fire service during the war and he remained at the temporary station in Springfield Road until sometime after the war had finished. His wife, my Aunt Doris, was appointed manager of the shop as the owner, Jack Jeffreys, was away in the Army.

I managed to get a Saturday morning job at Jeffreys' for the princely sum of 2 shillings. I did get a little knocked off any purchases but it was real slave labour. I had to sweep and wash the two front entrances to the shop before they were opened at either 8.30 or 9.00 a.m., go to the back store and undo the various packages ready for pricing, dispose of the rubbish, tidy up the tie counter, clean the changing rooms, get the coffee from across the road at Williamson's and go to the bank with the previous days takings. Then I would get out my bike and take the alterations to Mrs. Bass in New Writtle Street and bring some back before being sent to the stock room upstairs for tidying up.

Only on rare occasions was I allowed to serve, and that was usually on the tie counter, particularly at Christmas time. I enjoyed the stock room which, apart from clothes, was also the store for the window display dummies, price tickets and other displays. It must have been a jewellers shop before Jeffreys took over because I found many drawers of watch glasses and other jewellery items which nobody wanted. I was able to make a bit on the side by selling these to other members of the family. I don't remember the names of all the sales assistants but one named Smith was very kind to me and helped out many times.

Hunts the builders came next to Jeffreys. They sold everything a plumber or builder required and had a little alleyway next to their shop which led to the riverbank. Mr. Seabrook was the manager and he lived next door to my Uncle Ernest the Bootmaker in Lynmouth Avenue. He let me use the yard adjacent to the shop so that I could fish in the River Can. Kay's grocer was alongside followed by the Home and Colonial Stores and then Green's the spectacle manufacturers. This shop was managed by Mr. Cutts who was regarded as one of the best opticians in town. His daughter Audrey used to work with me in the Town Clerk's Office. She later married Ernest Collister, an architect in the town.

The Maypole store was further along and here my Aunt Doris had some rapport with the manager as I was often sent round to get the extra bit of butter which was wrapped in brown paper. Osborne's the tobacconist was next selling real briar pipes and a fantastic range of tobaccos.

Fox the hatter had a small shop next to Greens. This was run by an Alderman of the Council, Freddy Fox, an awesome man with a grey beard. However he allowed me to deliver his council documents to the shop rather than to his house in the Moulsham area. On official occasions, he looked magnificent in his council robes and cocked hat. These robes were on display at the back of his shop.

Adjacent was Webber's the jewellers. This was their main shop as they had another in Duke Street near the Cathedral. Mr. Webber the owner was a small stocky figure who was well known in the town. He lived in Broomfield at a place called "Brownings".

Nearby came the Queen's Head Hotel with access at the side to the boats which could be hired for trips up the river Can. Currys had a cycle store the other side. This was a long narrow shop and they sold mainly bicycles, batteries and other accessories.

The next shop along was the London Central Meat Company followed by Johnson the Dyers and Cleaners.

Next door was the large hardware shop of Luckin-Smith's. This was a super store and they sold everything: pots, pans, baskets, knives, forks and spoons. The manager was a short rotund Mr. Harrington. All the assistants wore long green coats and were ruled with a rod of iron by one Miss King. She was a giant of a woman - well over 6ft 6ins tall - and was a member of the well-known King family from Writtle. Her nephew Dick was a good cricketer against whom I played many times. Her niece Margaret was a secretary at Marconi's in the International Division and I knew her through my business activities at the firm. Halford's the cycle shop was adjacent.

Gosling's the shoe shop was further along. They sold high-class shoes. Next door was Cass's cycle repair shop. On many occasions I took my bike here for repair. The manager was a Mr. Licence - I used to go to school with his son Norman.

There was a passage adjacent to this shop which led to the second floor Conservative Club where my father took me when he played snooker. Nobby Clarke was the steward and he allowed me to play when nobody else was around. However I did not like this place as I often felt sick due to the heavy smoky atmosphere. Alongside was Montague Burton's followed by Rego the tailors and the department store of W.G. Wenley and Sons. This was a very large store and I remember one person in particular who worked there. He was Captain Robert Wenley who later became head of the local St. John Ambulance Brigade.

Bolingbroke's dress shop with a very large frontage came next. It was reckoned that the gentry of the time had all their dresses made here. Stanley Bolingbroke was the overseer and his son Wray ran the shop. Stanley Bolingbroke was an Alderman of the Council and he would not permit me to leave his council papers at the shop. Instead, I had to cycle all the way up Arbour Lane to his house, "The Brambles", right at the end.

Alongside Bolingbroke's, which also had an entrance at the rear in London Road, was another store of Oliver Parker - Luckin-Smith's, a provisions store, later taken over by Buttons.

The island on the corner, now fully occupied by Lloyds bank, was the headquarters of both Lloyds and Clarke's the booksellers and stationers. I spent many happy hours in this two storey building browsing through books and choosing paints for my water colour work.

London Road came next and this is where Samuel the Jewellers now stands. On this corner was a sweet shop and a greengrocers by the name of Peachey. I was coming along here one day during the war when a car driven by a lady got out of control. It mounted the pavement and crashed into Peachey's shop. Unfortunately a lady was either killed or maimed as one of her limbs was laying on the ground as I passed by.

Underground public toilets were behind the shop, on the Tindal Street Side and these were followed by the Chambers of the Norwich Union Insurance Company, Messrs. Wheeler and Illife Dental Surgeons, Fuller's the mens clothing shop, Woodward's the tailors and Leonard's Boot and Shoe Shop.

As we move up the High Street towards the Shire Hall the biggest shop was Smith's the Drapers who had another entrance in Tindal Street. The manager was a Mr. Perry, a homely, short, bald gentleman with a large moustache. He was a darling to the ladies and gave them adequate measure when cutting the rolls of materials. Seats were provided for tired customers or their children. I had to spend many a boring hour here whilst my mother chose some material for her dresses. One of the attractions in this shop was the miniature armchair in the basement which was used for displaying the creations.

Duttons the Printers had their entrance adjacent. Although much of the printing was done upstairs, the shop catered for the sale of blank pads and other stationery. Mr. Humphreys was the manager. He was a really grumpy man who did not like to be bothered with these small requirements.

Sainsbury's were alongside. Here the staff wore black coats and white aprons. Everybody shopped at Sainsbury's. The white marble counters, the highly polished brass scales and the legs of hams on porcelain stands stood out in my memory. Also the flying cups which were sent to the cashier at the end and returned with the customers' change. I don't remember the manager's name but he was a very helpful person.

Smaller shops were further alongside, they were Burney's who sold ladies gowns, Early Bunn Chemists and ladies hairdressers, solicitors offices of Messrs. Copland, Darby and Burrell, and then came the main offices of the Essex Chronicle, the leading local paper run by the Thompson family. The owner was Alderman J. Ockleford Thompson who, with his wife and family, was killed by an enemy bomb at their house in New London Road during the war.

The firm moved to Westway and for many years one of the sons was the manager. The Midland Bank was on the corner and was the last building in the street.

Whilst in the High Street it is worth noting that my mother was once manageress of a shop next to Sainsbury's, more recently owned by Sacks and Brendlor the furriers. It was called the Domestic Bazaar and sold mainly china and glass. One day a load of heifers were being driven from the railway goods yard, up New Street to the cattle pens in Market Road. One of the heifers escaped and ran down the High Street and yes, straight into the china shop where it caused a lot of damage before being removed. My mother's younger brother Robert was hastily called from his school to help clear up the mess which was not only china and glass.

One of the characters of the High Street before my time was according to my parents a policeman nicknamed "Krushen". He was on point duty opposite the Queen's Head Hotel near Springfield Road corner and stood by the Conduit which has now been removed to Admirals Park at the west end of town.

"Krushen" was apparently very precise in his actions and obtained the nickname after the then laxative known as "Krushen" Salts. Another policeman during and soon after the war was one P.C. Lamb, affectionately called Larry. He operated in a similar manner to P.C. "Krushen" but at the London Road entrance.

The High Street was the centre of the carnival processions held on the first Saturday in July when all the proceeds went to the Chelmsford and Essex Hospital in New London Road. For many years a Mr. Fewell, who ran a milk business, dressed up as John Bull and led the procession.

The High Street had buses going both ways as well as horses and carts and some street traders at certain times of the year, and, as today, a number of buskers particularly with tin whistles and piano accordions, even a barrel organ with a monkey at the London Road corner.

CHELMSFORD. DUKE STREET.

# Chapter Three

# DUKE STREET

Starting from the western end was Rainsford House, the home of the Chelmsford Borough Council Offices. It was a large house with three floors and an attic. The ground floor housed mainly the Treasurer's Department run by a Mr. George Leach,. second floor the Town Clerk's Department and part of the old Gas Office, third floor Borough Engineer's, and in the attic, the maintenance people.

There were some characters at this place. The caretaker was a Mr. Canfer. He hated anybody interrupting his daily routine. In the attic was a Mr. Bundock who regularly took a basket to this area. It took me a long time to find out the contents of this basket. Eventually it turned out to be racing pigeons. Mr. Bundock was a pigeon fancier and trained his pigeons from the roof of Rainsford House.

WAR MEMORIAL & RAINSFORD HOUSE CHELMSFORD.

At the back of the building were some garages and the local clinic whose overseer was a Dr. Mervyn Thomas, better known as the school doctor. In his clinic was the school dentist, a Mr. Maguire. Most school children hated coming to Mr. Maguire's clinic and the dreaded gas anaesthetic.

It was in the yard of Rainsford House that I learnt to drive a car. Due to the war, the cars were left in a garage as petrol was scarce. However one of the staff managed to undo a garage and get an old Austin Ruby onto the forecourt where I was taught to drive without going on to the road.

Adjacent to Rainsford House is the Chelmsford War Memorial first erected in memory of those who died in the 1914-18 war and now also dedicated to those lost in the 1939-45 war. Nowhere does it record the names of those who died which is a great pity, as most other war memorials do. It is impossible to find a collective list in Chelmsford of those brave people who gave up their lives in these two terrible conflicts.

The Borough Library, Council Chamber and Committee rooms were next. The Librarian in those days was Mr. Eric Reed and the caretakers Mr. Hilliard and his wife. One of my jobs was to take all the current papers for Council and Committee meetings to this building and also the files to the store beneath.

Not too many people used the library in those days. The tramps and other people with nothing else to do came into the Reading Room for the daily glance at the papers and, also to get a bit of warmth. The Mayors parlour was on the first floor and the secretary to the Mayor was Mr. Alan Hay, a very efficient character who organised all the Mayor's activities.

Across Fairfield Road came the Eastern National Bus Station. Single and double decker buses conveyed passengers all over Chelmsford and its surrounds. The manager was a Mr. Banks who was a friend of my father. Incidentally, I had a deaf and dumb Uncle who worked there as a painter. He was Walter Garnham Turrall (better known in sporting circles as "Pimpy").

Outside the first Viaduct near the Railway Bridge, were toilets and on the other side, a flower sellers stall. Under the bridge and on the Park Road corner was the Railway Tavern, often frequented by people travelling on the railway and buses.

The Friends' Meeting House was next although, this was not used as such but housed the Central Youth Club run by a Mr. Stan Precious. Cannon's Restaurant was alongside. This was a really top class restaurant and was used at weekends and some evenings for super dances. Boatman's the opticians run by Mr. Piper stood on the Victoria Road South corner. Above was the Prudential Insurance Company and the offices of the Friends' Provident Society.

Across the road right on the other corner was the booking office of Messrs. Rose Brothers, probably the only private coach and taxi operators in the area and in great demand to take people on holidays, theatre trips and outings. Mr. Rose lived in Widford Grove near my parents' house.

Next was Messrs. Gepp the Solicitors. Mr. Gepp was the Sheriff of the county. I knew one of the staff, Mr. Don Eagle, as he was a friend of my father's. A bit further along were other solicitors offices, Messrs Stunt and Leonard Gray. At the time it was understood that the partners of Leonard Gray and Alfred Darby had much to do with the sale of land and property in the Chelmsford area. Mr. Kenneth Burrell of Leonard Gray was a very kind man and on the occasions I visited him with my then small son, he always gave him 2/6d - half-a-crown in old money - 12 1/2p nowadays.

County Hall, the Headquarters of Local Government in Essex, was the biggest building in the street. This housed Public Health, Licensing, Education, Architects, Land Agency, Treasurer and County Clerks and many other departments. My father was a member of the Licensing Department and I had an evening job there selling newspapers to the staff. After school hours I collected my papers from the area in front of the Corn Exchange, and made around 2/6d per week for doing this.

The caretaker was a Mr. Runcorn who was a member of the King's Bodyguard, Yeomen of the Guard, and on many official occasions he was called to London to wear his brightly coloured Tudor uniform.

The Golden Fleece Public House and Restaurant was across the passage now called Threadneedle Street and this was frequently used by people attending the Friday market. Regular horse sales took place on the last Friday of each month and the travelling fraternity used the yards at the back of the "Fleece" to do a spot of bargaining, spitting into their hands and shaking hands on a deal.

Achille Serre the cleaners were adjacent followed by Messrs Godfrey's Sports shop and Saltmarsh the Nurseryman who sold fresh flowers and plants.

The Gas showrooms, run then by the Borough Council, was next managed by a Mr. George Norris. This is the place where local residents came to pay their gas bills.

Coming back on the opposite side of Duke Street to the West End we come to a Grocery Store run by Luckin-Smith's, the adjacent Bellamy's the Chemist, Hawkes Sweet Shop, Green the Greengrocer, and then Thompson the Bakers, which later became the Post Office run by Mr. Thompson, who, in his spare time, played a lot of water polo in the outdoor pool at Chelmsford and also at Clacton.

Michael Johns had their hairdressers shop alongside a narrow passage followed by a small bread and cake shop run by Shedd Brothers and then a very active tobacconists shop owned by Rippons, operated by two sisters. One Mrs. Wicks, was the spokesperson for all who entered therein. Her husband Ernest was the secretary of the Chelmsford Angling Club. Her sister was Kate Mee whose husband Stan was also a keen fisherman.

Cramphorn's corn and seed merchants had a shop adjacent then came Gramlick Jewellers and W and H.O. Budd the well known bakers. The best greengrocery in the town was at the next shop run by Mr. Harvey who travelled to Covent Garden every day to get fresh fruit and vegetables.

Baxfield's the fish shop was alongside. Miss Baxfield and her brother ran this shop. They always had a plentiful supply of fresh fish which they collected daily from the railway station. In those days they did not have refrigerated slabs and the only way to keep the fish cool was to have large pieces of ice around them. Ice came in large blocks and very often I have seen men unloading the ice which was wrapped in sack cloth. These days this would be considered most unhygienic.

Hoy's sweet shop was a place where you could find every type of sweet imaginable. Mr. Hoy who had a beard almost down to his waist, ran the shop helped by his daughter. He lived not far from my present home and he was a real character who would often advise on the state of the weather, forecasting the details by country methods which he had noted for many years. He was a tough character who would not use modern forms of transport and he walked to and from his shop each day.

One of the most sought after photographers following the era of Fred Spalding was E. Nixon-Payne who had his shop and studio adjacent. When I got married in September 1954 Mr. Payne took all our wedding photographs including a beautiful large colour photograph of Jean my wife. This was on display in his shop window for many weeks until I persuaded him to let me purchase it for my wife's birthday the following April.

Parkinson the Chemist was next door. Mr. Parkinson and his wife were always in the shop accompanied by their son John who, later took over the business. John was a member of the Galleywood Badminton Club of which I was Captain for many years. He later moved his business to Great Baddow.

A Co-operative Grocery Store was the next main shop and last before Wells Street was the old headquarters of the A.R.P. (Air Raid Precautions) across Wells Street on the corner was one of Hugh Wright's many butchery shops.

Mr. Wright was also a senior member of the Town Council and lived in a large house at the top end of Springfield Road. He too would not allow me to put his Council papers in any of his shops. Mr. Wright was a very good supporter of the Chelmsford City Football Club and when the City wished to sign on a player from another club, Mr. Wright often offered them jobs as butchers, as the players usually were only part time professionals. One I can remember was Ben Burley who played for many years at outside left for the City. Another was Dick Bell who eventually managed the Wright's butchers shop on the Broomfield Road Parade. Next shop along was Castle Cleaners followed by Finch's shoe shop.

A good meeting place for many people was the Bluebird Cafe adjacent to the butchers. This was owned by Mr. Christian Verdult. He was a member of the Borough Council and later became Mayor. Next came Newcombe's Cycles, Catling's Cafe and then the Chelmsford Dry Cleaners.

The Plough Hotel and Public House followed. Under the Railway Bridge was the Railway Station and Smith's Bookstall where outside was the taxi rank and the various paper sellers. I can remember on many Saturday evenings my father sent me on my bike to the railway station at 7 p.m. to pick up "The Green Un", the Ipswich paper produced only on a Saturday evening and containing all the football results and details of East Anglian teams.

*Great Eastern Railway Station. Chelmsford.*

Across the Station yard was the County Motor Works main showroom and repair garage. The manager for many years was Mr. Stan Shead. The owners were the Austin Brothers. Both these gentlemen were ex Military Officers and they also owned the County Hotel at the far end of Rainsford Road. On the corner was Hawkes the sweet shop. I have often queued here to buy their home made humbugs. Over Victoria Road was a big house, a dentists surgery run by Mr. Jones and later Mr. Russell. Taylor Walker had their wine shop adjacent followed by Rose Bros Coach Garage. Next was the "Animals" as the public house was affectionately known. It was the Lion and Lamb Hotel which had at the rear one of the best dance halls in the county. All the up-market annual functions were held here plus many conferences and wedding receptions.

A number of passageways were further along the road, one of which housed Shergolds the printers. They produced in the main posters, raffle tickets and headed paper. The Cedar Cafe followed and then J.C. Pawson solicitor. Mr. Pawson was an Alderman of the Borough and I often left his council papers at his office. He was the old type of solicitor who had piles of documents on his desk and employed a clerk with one of those very high desks with a quill and ink stand. A.W. Andrews Funeral Furnishers were also on this side. Their main parlour and reception area was in the front, all beautiful boarded panels with a small office at the back. The embalming parlour was accessed from New Street along the railway siding. They also kept their cars in this area.

Alderman Arthur W. Andrews was the owner. He was a jolly rotund gentleman who always wore a Homburg and black jacket and striped trousers. He eventually was Mayor of Chelmsford and was extremely kind to me in my short career with the Borough Council. He allowed me to leave the council papers at his Duke Street office. I later found out that he was a very good friend of my father and was a senior person associated with the Essex County Football Association. He was later helped in the practice by his daughter Peggy and her husband John Jordan.

County Typewriters had their offices nearby run by Miss Hilda Sorrell. Many young ladies in the town have started their career at the hands of Hilda. She was very well known for her ability to train young ladies in the best skills of typing. She also employed people who took on contracts for typing work for the various firms in the town as the luxury of photo-copying did not exist in those days.

Adjacent to the Funeral Furnishers were Fred Taylor and Co Auctioneers. The business was run by a Mr. A.G. Wilks who, being an ex Army gentleman, advised everybody that he should be known as Major Wilks. He lived in the same village as my parents - Widford, and was known as the local squire. His son Anthony was also in the business which is now owned by Black Horse Agencies. At the rear of the premises was a large auction room. Many a day I have stood in there whilst my mother bid for one of the sales

Duke Street, Chelmsford

items. It became my duty to transport whatever she bought on my bicycle or alternatively, to get the local horse and cart delivery man to get the larger items home.

After Taylors was the Castle's Wine Merchants premises, followed by Slipper's Auctioneers, Low and Low Accountants and then Wisemans the Architects.

Further along was the Amber Tea Rooms. This was what we might now call a fast food restaurant. Many people frequented this place to obtain a quick bite to eat. Almost adjacent was Webber's the jewellers. This was the second of their shops and run by a very kind gentleman whose spare time duty was that of a member of the Special Constabulary. Mr. Webber was a short stocky gentleman with a ginger moustache. He spent time in both of his shops. He lived in Broomfield Road in a house called "Brownings". This is now demolished, and an associated field now contains a modern housing estate.

To many a young boy the smell of ground coffee meant a visit next door to Harrison's the Grocers. They had a coffee machine with a window open to the road. The smell of the coffee wafted into Duke Street and those standing in the bus queues adjacent to the Cathedral had the benefit of this wonderful smell.

Just past the Cathedral opening was Batson the Typewriter Company, Scott's the Printers and Ward's Book Shop then a small shop for repairing watches and clocks. This was run by a very kind gentleman, Mr. Kraft who I think came from one of the East European countries.

# Chapter Four

# TINDAL SQUARE AND THE SHIRE HALL

A nearby passageway led to the Cathedral before an office housing Cobbe and Wincer local land agents. Ingalls were next who sold mainly gentlemen's high class and hand made shoes. This place was often visited by the upper-class. Next door was Godfrey's. This shop sold everything to do with leatherwear plus camping, fishing and other outdoor activities. Their main premises were in Moulsham Street where a large tent and marquee manufacturing business was carried out. The owner was a Mr. J.B. Godfrey who was also a Borough Councillor. He was one of the few shop owners who allowed me to leave his council papers in his shop rather than take them all the way up Moulsham Street to his residence known as "Corbiere".

Bellamy's the chemists came next. This was a sister shop to the one at the West End of Duke Street. The owner was Mr. Tom Bellamy, another Borough Councillor who eventually became an Alderman and later Mayor of Chelmsford. He lived in Springfield Road and, yes, I had to deliver his council papers to his residence and not his shop.

Debnam's the hairdressers was the shop adjacent to the main entrance to the Cathedral grounds. This shop was the place where the "uppercrust" of the town had their hair or hair pieces trimmed together with their moustaches. They were very expensive and I can remember one Mr. Jewell being the manager or owner. He was connected with local football and probably was one time a director of the Chelmsford City Football Club in New Writtle Street.

On the other side of the Cathedral passage is the Shire Hall. This magnificent building is probably regarded as the centre piece of the town and has a very good sprung dance hall. For many years it was the seat of justice before the Crown Court was built in New Street. It was stated that prisoners in cells at the local "nick" on the corner of New Street and Waterloo Lane, were transported under the road to the Shire Hall by a passage which led directly to one of the courts.

SHIRE HALL, CHELMSFORD.

Many a time have I seen the carriages arriving with beautiful ladies and their escorts for one of the magnificent dances held in the Shire Hall ballroom. The Hunt Ball was always held there and the Town Ball. In later life I was privileged to be one of the escorts to ladies attending the Town Ball - a most expensive occasion.

Almost opposite the Shire Hall was the statue to one of Chelmsford's famous sons, Sir Nicholas Tindal who was born in Moulsham Street and became the Lord Chief Justice of England. Behind the statue was a horse trough where on many occasions I saw the last of the carts pull up to allow their thirsty horses a drink.

Across the way was another of Chelmsford's famous landmarks, the Corn Exchange. Due to misguided plans by the local authorities, in the 1960's the Corn Exchange was demolished together with the famous street of many pubs known as Tindal Street, sometimes called "Back Street".

The Corn Exchange housed the many stalls where on a Friday local farmers came to offer their corn to other buyers. My own grandfather Thomas W. Turrall who was a corn and seed merchant from Kelvedon, had one of these stalls and was a regular figure at the Corn Exchange on a Friday. Later on his eldest son Willy carried on the tradition.

At other times, the Corn Exchange was used for many events. Bazaars, meetings, skating, wrestling and boxing matches as well as wonderful dances. Many a Chelmsford couple met at these dances and later married.

Outside and in the little alcoves at the front, sat two well known characters selling newspapers. One was Bob Bailey who sold the Evening Standard and the other was Mr. Flack who sold the Evening News. Mr. Flack had one of those tricycles with a big box on the front. He lived somewhere in the Corporation Road area. Many a time I have collected the papers from this area and sold them in County Hall after I had been to school. In those days you could leave your bicycle and the money for the papers anywhere, in the sure knowledge that they would still be there when you returned.

Let us now wander down Tindal Street. The first pub was The Bell. It housed a wonderful rear yard which later on was used as the Chelmsford open air market after the normal market in Market Road was being moved. Often on a Saturday morning my mother would deposit me on the seat in The Bell yard whilst she took, as she said, light refreshment within.

There were many pubs in this area including The Spotted Dog run by one Mrs. Cheney. She was a well built lady who often put her presence on the pavement outside her pub with her hands on her hips announcing that hers was the best run pub in the street.

Other places in the street were Driver's the Printers. Pope and Smiths,

*Chelmsford, Tindal Street.*

who ran a sports outfitters shop both owners being Essex cricketers. Peter Smith was an excellent bowler and also played for England. He had a cousin Ray who was also an excellent bowler but was not in the business. There was the odd yard in the area and a Cafe known as "The Cottage" run, by Mr. And Mrs. Chivers. This place sold wonderful home made pies and served delightful meals. Further on was the Army and Navy Stores selling mostly ex-service clothes which were quite cheap to buy.

Further down the road was a Corn and Seed Merchants, G.B. Ling, later owned by Cramphorns. Adjacent was Poney's the bakers. They were Chelmsford's finest bakers and their Hovis brown bread was a speciality. I remember that the owner's wife, Mrs. Frank Poney, was a very erect lady with her hair done in a bun. She served in the shop wearing her black dress and immaculate white lace apron. Later in life, I had the pleasure of knowing her daughter Margaret who also served in the shop. Mr. Frank Poney set up a club to assist disadvantaged people of the town which later became the Chelmsford St. Raphael Club for Physically Handicapped people. Mr. Poney's daughter Margaret Gay, later on ran this Club until she died in 1993. This club is still very active.

Also in this street were the Dolphin Inn, Leeches Gunsmiths, Mansfield Butchers (who I believe took over from Hugh Wright), Walton Mens' Outfitters, Cook Wine Merchants, Barlow Artists' materials, Budd the Baker and McNair Ladies Hairdressers, Hasler & Hance, Ironmongers.

Right on the corner of Tindal Street also fronting London Road was Wainwrights Milk Bar. This was also the start of one of Chelmsford's Fast Food Bars. The younger element of the town frequented this place especially on a Saturday. It became the meeting place where many a friendship was formed.

Tindal Street still exists but has lost all its interesting shops and pubs, which have been replaced by the blank wall of the new Boots.

From Tindal Square to the High Street behind what was Clarke's Bookshop and is now Lloyds Bank runs the very short narrow Conduit Street, so called I suppose because it led eventually to the conduit which used to stand at Springfield Road corner.

ENTHRONEMENT OF FIRST BISHOP OF
CHELMSFORD, 23rd APRIL, 1914.

# Chapter Five

# ST. MARY'S PARISH CHURCH - CHELMSFORD CATHEDRAL AND NEW STREET

Situated in the heart of Chelmsford and behind the Shire Hall, is the Cathedral, formerly St. Mary's, the Parish Church of Chelmsford which in the early part of the century was a sleepy market town with a population of some thirty thousand people. Now the boundaries have changed and Chelmsford boasts a population of over 150,000.

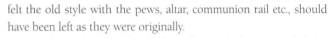

If you examine some of the early photographs of both the inside and outside of this church which became a Cathedral in the early part of last century, you will notice a tremendous change. Inside, the Cathedral has been completely refurbished with all the old pews, font and pulpits removed and the altar area updated. In more recent times the old organ was removed and two new organs installed, one in the Choir area and the other in the Nave area. The Cathedral has a more light and open feeling though many people felt the old style with the pews, altar, communion rail etc., should have been left as they were originally.

Outside in the churchyard the railings which surrounded the many pathways have been removed and a number of the gravestones and monuments are nowhere to be seen.

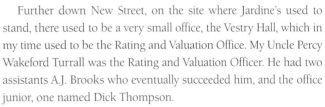

Further down New Street, on the site where Jardine's used to stand, there used to be a very small office, the Vestry Hall, which in my time used to be the Rating and Valuation Office. My Uncle Percy Wakeford Turrall was the Rating and Valuation Officer. He had two assistants A.J. Brooks who eventually succeeded him, and the office junior, one named Dick Thompson.

At some time I had to go to this office to collect my employment badge, enabling me to do a paper round in Chelmsford, as all young people undertaking part time employment whilst still at school, had to be registered. I remember being interviewed by the schools inspector in these offices, a Mr. Murphy. A genial man with Salvation Army connections, he had the task of visiting parents if their child failed to attend school for any length of time. The cleaner at Vestry Hall was one May Say - more about her later.

The King William IV Public House was the only the second licensed premises in this road and this eventually closed down, but the frontage still remains as part of the modern new development there.

Then came a number of offices and a shop owned by the Chamberlains. This shop sold everything you could think of in the way of new or second-hand novelties. Mr. Chamberlain was an old man with grey hair which seemed to stand on end as if he had been given an electric shock. He was a hard bargainer when you wanted to sell an item and even harder when you wanted to buy something. However the shop was fascinating and, on many occasions I bought postage stamps, caps for my gun and Guy Fawkes masks.

Then came Legg Street in which was housed a small timber yard run by Bloomfields. Here you could pick up a bargain with some of the finest wood available. I remember just after the war the main wood sold which was a very durable one was called Ramin. A little further along was the Self-Motoring garage, which was a motor repair business and had all night availability of petrol and oil. This was right next to the Wheatsheaf Pub frequently used by the many people working at the major industries of Hoffmans and Marconi's.

Opposite the pub, and on the site of the new police station was a garage owned by Hadlers. This was another repair business. A very strict proprietor and manager was a Mr. Amey who would carefully examine and comment on any vehicle brought to the garage for repair. Various sweetshops and vegetable shops were adjacent and then an open space on which stood a small hut owned and lived in by the one and only May Say. I regret I do not know anything about her background, but, she appeared to live the life of a hermit only venturing out to swear at passers by and to clean the Vestry Hall offices. She used to lean over the fence where her abode was built with a "Mrs. Mop" type head scarf and a very large apron which started under her chin and ended near her shoes. Her face was always the colour of brown shoe polish and I am told she was one of Chelmsford's characters.

Next to May Say's residence was Guy Harlings, which is now the home of the Chelmsford Diocesan offices as well as the Cathedral offices. The Crown Courts are one side of Guy Harlings now and on the other side is Mayntrees which is still the "Judges' Lodgings" when they attend the Crown Court. The other houses are now office premises.

The last place on this side of the road is the old police station with its blue lamp still there. Many a time I have visited this place to obtain a dog licence or to return an item which had been found in the street.

Going back down New Street. On the site of the new police station stood Hawkes the sweet factory where many of the sweets bought in Essex shops were made. They had a fleet of vehicles to transport their confectionery and did a good line in humbugs.

Across Victoria Road and still into New Street were a few houses and corner shops before the old bridge. This bridge was a very small affair in comparison to the large bridge which carries the railway today. The bridge was originally built when horse and carts were the only mode of transport. When motor vehicles came along, especially omnibuses, there was real congestion as no two vehicles could pass through at the same time.

Under the bridge and on the left hand side is the Marconi factory. Known originally as the Wireless Telegraph and Signal Company in 1897. It later changed its name to Marconi's Wireless and Telegraph Company (MWTCO) and the site today is occupied by Marconi Mobile

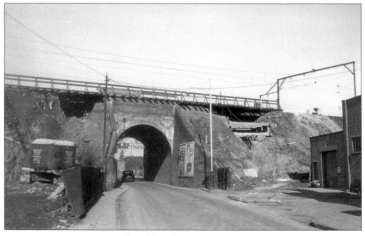

The Old Bridge in New Street

and also Alenia-Marconi. Most of my adult life was spent at this site where I started as a Draughtsman and rose to the position of Director Overseas Sales and eventually Manager of PR and Publicity before I retired in 1996.

I can remember when I first started in 1950 the number of employees was over 11,000 as opposed to the 500 today. Most of the men wore cloth caps and were always smoking - something which is very rare today. This was the headquarters of all Marconi's factories. As the product range increased the company was split up and now occupies many sites in the UK leaving only Mobile and Radar work at this site.

When I was a young lad, my father told me of the many activities which took place at Marconi's. This included an account of the day during the war when an enemy bomb hit the factory and a number of people were killed. On the roof of Marconi House was a Bofor Gun under the control of one Captain Jimmy Michael of the Home Guard. He was an employee of the company and lived near my parents. On many occasions Captain Michael had a go at the enemy bombers flying over the site by firing the Bofor Guns.

The Marconi site occupied nearly 22 acres and behind the factory was a large brewery owned by Ridleys. Following a fire in the disused brewery, this site was eventually bought by the GEC-Marconi Company and the area is now partly a car park and partly new offices for the Alenia-Marconi Company. It was on this site that the early Marconi public broadcasts were made and the two 450ft radio masts were landmarks for miles around. Dame Nellie Melba the famous Australian soprano opera singer performed the first "on air" broadcast from New Street in the early 1920's but the very first voice "on air" from the New Street site was Winifred Sayers who later on, married a Mr. Felix Collins Head of the Special Constables during the 1940's. Winifred sang a song now long forgotten called "Absence".

Much history was made at this site, too much to include here. Originally the whole site was owned by the Church Commissioners and it was a cricket ground before Guglielmo Marconi decided to build a factory for manufacturing wireless equipment. For many years the cricket pavilion remained and was used as a table tennis area by Marconi employees.

Marconi Road is adjacent to the factory and on the corner stood Newcombe's the cycle shop. Here the very best cycles were obtained. I can remember my first new bicycle a very heavy Sunbeam came from this shop.

Various shops and houses followed before the famous factory and office block of the Hoffman Ball and Roller Bearing factory, which occupied a large part of the Rectory Lane and New Street site. Regrettably this factory, which employed at one time 15,000 people is no more. The site is now owned and magnificent buildings erected, by Anglia Polytechnic University. Globe House which at one time housed part of the Hoffman offices still stands and some of this building has recently been let out to small businesses., and some parts converted to flats.

The famous Chelmsford Railway Goods Yard stood between Globe House and the Railway bridge. This is where all goods traffic ended and Carter Paterson Horse Drawn and other vehicles moved the goods around Chelmsford. Also here were the arrival pens for cattle and sheep before the animals were driven up New Street to Chelmsford market. My Uncle Charles Turrall was for many years manager of the goods yard and I can remember going to his offices where there was a blazing fire with plenty of kettles boiling.

Uncle Charles was a very good footballer and cricketer. In football he once played for Tottenham Hotspur as an amateur. In those days if you were good at sport, employers wanted to take you on and offered you an excellent job. It gave them a lot of publicity to have a well known name in their employ. In this area were the coal yards of local traders Coote and Warren, the Co-op, Thomas Moy, Bullock and Clarke.

Just the other side of the old bridge stood the famous Suet factory.

Unfortunately this got burned down and the smell of the suet hung around for many weeks. The area is now occupied by Marconi as a store. Next comes the old Victoria Road School. In my time this was used as Marconi's Social Club, Company offices and later on as a store. The area behind is known as Driver's Yard. It was here the famous Bob Driver lived in a house called "The Laurels". Bob formed a Scrap Metal business with a Mr. Ling.

Referring to the Hoffman site, it housed one of the most modern Social Clubs with a wonderful dance hall where on many occasions I have taken part in either Olde Tyme or Modern dances. In addition I have often played badminton here.

# Chapter Six

# MARKET ROAD AND KING EDWARD AVENUE

## Market Road

This quaint little road, named for obvious reasons, had various shops and alleyways before reaching the market proper. From the Tindal Square end and opposite the side of the Corn Exchange was a little shop called Kents. This sold picture frames and mirrors and was run by an ex World War 1 veteran who was blinded in service to the country. His sister used to help in the shop and on many occasions she steered him round the town or out to visit his clients.

Lionel Cattle had a small tailor's shop adjacent. Many of the gentry used this shop as Mr. Cattle had a high reputation for his tailored suits. Adjacent was a public toilet before the next main building, on the corner of King Edward Avenue and Market Road. This housed Britain Pash, agricultural engineers, whose showrooms always displayed the latest tractors and mechanical farm implements.

Alas King Edward Avenue no longer exists but when you walk through the County Hall Atrium you still travel the same route from Threadneedle Street to Victoria Road.

Then came the market and market offices which were if I remember correctly, run by Alfred Darby, Hilliard and W.J. Slipper (no relation as far as I know to the famous copper who sought the great train robbers in the 1950's). These offices were occupied by staff to collect money from the buyers following the auction of animals and other items. On either side of these offices were the pens housing chickens, rabbits, pigeons and goats, and at Christmas time turkeys, either plucked or unplucked.

The Market, Chelmsford

One man stands out in my memory, this was Mr. Hammond. He was known as "Peaso" because with his horse and cart, he brought vegetables in season to the householders in the area and his favourite cry was "Peaso". He appeared to be an auctioneer's assistant and dressed in his khaki coat, he held up the animals for the auctioneer to obtain a bid. Many a time an animal escaped from his clutches and "Peaso" would have to chase around the stalls to catch it for the auctioneer.

Day old chicks were always sold and I can see now the young faces peering into the boxes and asking their mums if they could buy one and take it home. They only cost one or two pence and on occasions particularly in the war years, my parents bought some of these chicks for rearing, egg laying and finally ending up on the Christmas Day table.

Opposite this area were the cattle and pig pens. This was a fairly extensive area stretching almost down to what we called the "Rec" - (recreation ground now renamed Central Park). The cattle were in open pens whilst the pigs and other small animals were in pens under cover. The auctioneer in this area used to walk along the boards above the animal pens and carry out his auction from on high. One day whilst I was watching the drovers marking the pigs for the auctioneer, the poor man slipped off the boards and landed in the pig sty. Not only was his face red when he eventually climbed back on the boards but his suit was covered in slippery slime and the smell was awful.

Close to the under cover pens was the local fire station. No fancy names - they were called the Chelmsford Fire Brigade, and had two engines parked in their station. All the men wore brass helmets when they went out to a fire. Adjacent to the fire station was a small toilet mainly used on market days.

A small street ran alongside the fire station known as Threadneedle Street (this conjures up some thoughts) there were a number of houses on one side of the road which led to the Recreation ground.

On market days, which were usually on a Friday, a number of stalls were erected opposite the fire station and down Threadneedle Street. The most significant of the stalls was the one run by Women's Institute. They always had a variety of home made goodies, jams, cakes, sweets and preserves and of course a lot of garden produce. I can still visualise these dear old ladies with their various shaped hats selling off their produce. Nowadays this would not be allowed and I suspect this is why we do not see any WI stalls at our new covered market which stands underneath the multi-storey car park on the site which was once our cattle market.

At the bottom end of the cattle market was the now demolished Drill Hall. This was the place where recruits in both the first and second World Wars assembled before going off to their various postings. As a National Serviceman I had to do five years training there and weekend camps in the summer following my two years military service on active duty. This building has now been replaced by the Royal and Sun Alliance headquarters.

CHELMSFORD MARKET 580

New Drill Hall, Chelmsford. 30.

LIBRARY, MUSEUM & ART SCHOOLS, CHELMSFORD. 660.

The Drill Hall led to what is now known as Victoria Road South in which was situated the Chelmsford Technical College and School of Art. A lot of my early education was spent here either at day or night classes. This now forms part of the Anglia University complex as the now defunct Technical School moved to Patching Hall Lane. The John Payne School now occupies the premises.

The Market Road Baptist Church came next followed by Eastern Garages where rather a lot of Austin cars were always on display on the forecourt.

Opposite Eastern Garages were the gardens of Gepp and Sons, Solicitors, whose main offices were in Duke Street. We can still see their magnificent Magnolia Tree which always seems to hail the start of summer when in bloom. A small building was next which at one time was a doctors' surgery. It was then used as an insurance office and called "Magnolia House". Next door on the site of the old market auction room stands the extension to County Hall and the magnificent library.

## Kind Edward Avenue

Alas this no longer exists. On one side was County Hall. It also housed the county library and the main entrance leading to the motor vehicle licensing offices and on the other side part of J. Britain Pash the agricultural engineers. Alongside this building were a number of private residences. Some of them were occupied as overflow offices for the Essex County Council and in one was the local registry office for births, marriages and deaths. It always amused me that this office, in particular for births and deaths, was only open for part of the day. Often this proved difficult for people to register their requirements and I wondered what the staff did for the rest of the day as the hours were something like 10 a.m. to 3 p.m. The new registry office is now part of the County Hall complex.

CHELMSFORD. MOULSTAM ST. & STONE BRIDGE.

Chapter Seven

# MOULSHAM STREET

The old stone bridge over the River Can is the start of Moulsham Street. Nowadays with the influx of motor vehicles, the charm and character of this lovely street has been severely tarnished as the street is virtually split in half by Parkway a four lane motorway.

Stone Bridge, Chelmsford

Body the Chemists occupied the corner building near the bridge and above them was the Pearl Insurance office. Adjacent Frank Miles the tailors. A small Hawkes sweet shop was next before coming to Rankin the drapers. This is the place where ladies were able to obtain their party dresses and also everyday wear. Another Chelmsford character frequented this place. His name was Jones and he was Rankin's errand boy. He always wore a grey suit and matching cap and rode a trade bicycle fitted with extra blocks on the pedals as he was so short. He had a bit of a stutter and very large protruding front teeth.

The famous Regent Theatre was adjacent where some wonderful shows were staged. I can remember the Matthews brothers running the place just after the war and I took part in some of the Chelmsford Operatic Society shows by looking after "The Limes" as they were called, these being the spotlights mounted on the balcony rails. The main shows which I covered were Annie Get Your Gun, Oklahoma and Brigadoon. The Matthews Brothers were involved with their parents in Marionettes and these were really quite fantastic shows.

Before reaching the corner stood Stapletons, a shop which sold everything to do with pork including chops, sausages, trotters and chaps - which were pigs' cheeks. Pigs' trotters were a delicacy but unfortunately they are no longer available. With plenty of vinegar, salt and pepper, in those days a pair of trotters formed a good meal.

Next to Stapletons was Turner the basket shop. It was a treat to see all the various shaped baskets which Mr. Turner hung outside his shop each day. They ranged from conventional shopping baskets to those which were used at Covent Garden for fruit and vegetables. He even had chairs made out of basket weave. No problems in those days with all the wicker work outside on the pavement. People were honest and would not steal any of these products neatly stacked in front of the shop.

Baddow Road fruiterers were on the corner run by the Harris family. Opposite and still there, Loveday the jewellers. W. And O. Budd the bakers were adjacent to Loveday's. They had a bakery in Springfield Road but all the local area deliveries were made from this shop. Yet another dry cleaners was adjacent run by Castles. Ryder's the upmarket toy shop came next. It was here all young boys and girls saw their dream toys in the window. I used to look through the windows just before Christmas and tried to persuade my parents to buy the toys I wanted. Ryders were about the only shop in Chelmsford during those days to sell the pram carriages such as Marmet and Swallow.

A small radio shop run by Flexmans was alongside. It was here many Chelmsford people bought their very first radio and later television sets. Just before the second world war Flexmans had a demonstration of the Baird TV System with the rotary discs and lights showing various figures on the screen. The well known Windmill Inn and Public House was next door.

W. Ralph Catt, high class grocer, occupied the adjacent building. The Windmill Public House had a rather large yard alongside. Two further shops, Fulchers an excellent florist and then another of Bellamy's chemist shops. Mr. Tommy Grew the pawnbroker's shop was next and then a pair of houses one of which was later turned into a pet shop. These last mentioned buildings had to make way for the Parkway ring road.

Just past here were a number of shops. I particularly remember Churchill Johnson the builders' merchants, Warren the children's outfitters, Helen Eldridge ladies hairdresser, Mathews greengrocers, Frank Poney's cake, pastry

Moulsham St., Chelmsford.

Moulsham Street, Chelmsford

and bread shop and another called "The Bungalow". This was a small sweet shop run by two dear old ladies whose names were the Misses Bedford. Right next door was the Citadel of the Chelmsford Salvation Army. In comparison to their current modern building in Baddow Road this was very small. Nevertheless they always raised the roof with their resounding war cry and the noise from the band.

Hall Street came next and on the corner was another sweet shop called Bucks, a rather grumpy Mr. Buck ran the shop and he was not at all pleased to see young boys asking for their pennyworth of sweets on a Saturday morning.

The shops alongside changed hands many times and memories cannot cope with these. One shop I do remember on this side sold horsemeat. It was run by a Mr. Palmer and I feel certain on numerous occasions during the war, we ate some of this horsemeat. Rippons the newsagents were a bit further along the road and for some short time I had a paper round here before moving further along the road to Jones paper shop as they offered more money.

Yet another public house the Kings Arms. A Mrs. Parsons was the landlady and her son Philip was a school friend of mine. This was followed by yet another of the Luckin-Smith's shops, Bell the chemist, Parish the fruiterer and greengrocer and then Denison's cycles. Mr. Denison was a very small man but had terrific strength. With one hand he could pull the tyre off a bicycle wheel without the use of the conventional tyre levers. He was ably assisted in the shop by his sister.

A milliners shop run by Miss Smee was next, then Lodge's the fruiterers, McKnay the hairdresser, Jones' paper shop and then Godfrey's rope works. It was there that many of the tents and marquees were made for the big shows and upper-class wedding feasts.

Well we have nearly reached St. John's church and thereafter there were no more shops but private residences. Even the St. John's school adjacent to the church was empty except for occasional use during the second world war.

Returning now to the other side of the road near the Stone Bridge, the first shop on the corner was Foster's the gents' and boys' outfitters. Here my parents bought my standard grey flannel trousers and shirts for school wear. Phillips had a shoe shop next door. The International Grocery Stores stood adjacent run by a very jovial manager Mr. Gaze. Plattin the chemist had the next shop. Many times have the older generation visited and taken their offspring to this shop. Mr. Horace Plattin who died at nearly 100 years old was as good as any doctor and was able to diagnose ills and offer a remedy. His sister and a Mr. Clements were assistants in this shop.

The Co-op Boot and Shoe Shop was next and this was run by a very genial man Mr. Ridgewell. My father always purchased his boots from this shop.

On the corner of Barrack Square were a number of outlets run by the Co-op including their main grocery department. On the other side of Barrack Square and in Moulsham Street was Bonds furnishing store. This was a really big up market place with a wide selection of lounge, kitchen and bedroom furniture. The London Drapery Stores were alongside then a small greengrocery shop run by Greenwoods and adjacent a wet fish shop owned by Roebucks. They sold some of the finest haddock and cod seen in the town. Mrs. Roebuck who lived in upper Moulsham was a great friend of my mother. A photographic studio run by Charles Limited was next door.

Hugh Wright the butcher ran the next shop along. Friends of mine, Albert and Betty East were the children of the landlord and I went to school with them. Their parents were very kind to me and I often stayed to have tea with them.

Masons the newsagents and booksellers were the next main shop and this was managed by a dear old boy Mr. Tunstall. He was a real fuss pot and everything in the shop had to be just so. I did have a paper round with the shop for sometime. Just round the corner was Royce the ladies hairdressers and next to them the Moulsham fruiterers.

Then came a road called the Friars and on the opposite corner was the Bata shoe shop. They sold inexpensive shoes which, in those days, most people could afford. Another dry cleaner, Campbell Garrick with an enormous steam ironing board in the window was followed by the Cash Domestic Store.

The family firm of Green the butchers sold the choicest meat. I often had to go here and collect my mothers weekly ration of beef or lamb and sometimes liver. Mr. Green ran the shop and his wife served in the cash desk. Ken Gardener was one of the butchers and he always gave me a little bit extra meat. I realised then why my mother sent mince pies and home-made wine at Christmas for the staff.

Martyn Green the son was learning the trade and his fiancee eventually went into the cash desk. Martyn got married and after his fathers death carried on the business for sometime before retiring to farm at Widford.

Smaller shops along the way have escaped my memory but there was one called Souths who sold fried fish and chips. The entrance was down a slope and all the fish and chips they sold were wrapped up in newspaper.

An amusement arcade was close by. Many a time I have gone inside and spent my coppers in an effort to beat the machines. I never did and came out convinced they were rigged.

A second-hand and antiques shop run by "Pony" Moore had everything you could think of from furniture down to pram wheels. He, Mr. Moore was a hoarder. His windows were filled with what I thought was junk and it appeared nothing ever moved from the shop although I suppose he must have made a living. His two sons were known to me from schooldays and later on one of them, Stanley, came to work at the same firm, Marconi's, where I spent nearly all my business life.

Stanley Jarmain's cycle shop was next door. This is where we took our bikes for repair, even for punctures until my mother's next door neighbour showed me how to repair a puncture with a kit which was not very expensive. After this Jarmain's only got my trade for ball bearings, batteries and later on a Miller dynamo. Rossington's green grocery store was next door. Ronald the son was a school friend of mine.

Migliorini's the ice cream shop was adjacent. They made the best ice creams in Chelmsford. I used to know their son Peter. They also had a very good looking daughter whose name I cannot recall.

Ted Temple's the barber shop was next door. It was here my father, my brother and myself had our haircuts. The cost was 1/6d. Ted Temple the boss had a son Gordon to whom he taught the business. In those days a number of men went there to be shaved, usually with a cut throat razor. A bookie's shop or "Turf Accountants" run by Frank Gillard was conveniently placed next door. Followed by Everett's the boot and shoe repairers and then the Sun Cafe.

Another pub, the Bay Horse came before a yard, on the other side of which was Rolph's the Fishmonger and then Batas shoe repair shop; Shedd the baker had a shop adjacent and then came a radio shop run by a Mr. F.E. Smith.

New Writtle Street had on its opposite corner a draper's shop, Denny selling mainly children's clothes then Angell a mens' outfitters and Howe's confectionery shop. The Moulsham Post Office run by the Powell family was nearby. Their son Derek in later life played badminton for "Chelmsford Casuals" and often we met on the opposite sides of the badminton court.

Many shops in Moulsham Street changed hands and memory does not allow me to name them all. However there was Brewsters selling second-hand furniture and other items, Gibson's furniture, Wilkinson's sweet shop, Ives the watchmaker and Shipp's sweets. Mrs. Shipp a fine figure of a woman often stood in the doorway with folded arms ready to pounce on any unsuspecting youngster to entice them to spend their pocket money in her shop.

Next door was Coomb's fish shop followed by French's bootshop, Candler the butcher and then Frear's hardware stores. If you wanted anything in the hardware line this was the place to go. Mr. Frear stocked anything from a paraffin wick right through to large dustbins and wheel barrows. His son John was a school friend and many an hour I have spent with him in his fathers hop.

Warminger's bookshop was next door, then came Tom Jarvis the greengrocer. Tom was in the Widford Church Choir with me, a robust but kind character. If he saw me passing he would often invite me into his shop and give me an apple or a pear. Whitley's electrical and Matthew's pork butchers shops were close by and the next largest place in the road was the British Restaurant where people could get a meal in wartime at a reasonable cost. This was followed by a quite large garage run by Lasts who specialised if I remember correctly in Wolsely cars.

The pubs along the way made this probably the street in Chelmsford with the second highest number of pubs. Among them the Bay Horse, Cricketers, Kings Arms, Windmill, Star and Garter and the Anchor. Some of them have already changed their names. The Kings Arms is now the Wig and Firkin.

Moulsham Street at the south end had a number of small cottages and then the Mildmay Alms houses before coming to the larger houses owned by the gentry of the time. Mr. Green the butcher and the Scott family. Mrs. Sandeman of Sherry fame lived on the corner of Southborough Road. As an innocent choirboy at Widford Church, I used to collect her in her very large bath chair and wheel her to the 11 a.m. service. Mrs. Sandeman gave me 2/6d each time I collected her. It soon became known that I had this mission and suddenly many other choirboys tried to get in on the act.

Nearby were houses owned by a Mrs. Windley and a Mrs. Gilbey. They appeared to be quite wealthy people. Opposite was a very kind man Mr. Dorwood, and next door to him lived the Wenley family.

Before the Dovedale College took it over I was often invited to the house owned by the Wells family who were well known brewers. They gave me many books to read and a lot of Chinese rice paper sketches which alas are no more and, doubtless now would be worth a lot of money.

My only other recollection of Moulsham Street is of a house at the top end near the roundabout, next to Highfield, now owned by St. John's Hospital as a nurses residence. This was the home of Miss Norah Taylor sister of Sidney C. Taylor, one time Mayor of Chelmsford. Norah was a friend of my mother and she had a large garden with a brick built summerhouse in which I played for many an hour.

Opposite her house was a piece of open ground. During the 1939-45 war this was used as a depot by the Government to make Wattle Fences as barricades to stop the German Army invasion of England. My father, mother, next door neighbour Mr. Gillam, and myself helped make these wattles. Often I would go wandering like any young boy would. In the same patch of ground I found several glass bottles filled with a red liquid. In sheer devilment I picked one up and threw it onto Princes Road whereupon it exploded and set the tarmac alight. My father soon put a stop to my antics and, as the local fire watcher, confiscated the remainder which he said were Molotov Cocktail bombs, probably dropped by a German bomber.

On the same side of the road were some very large houses one of which was taken over for use by the Marconi apprentices. It was known as Brooklands.

Chapter Eight

# NEW LONDON ROAD

I start this chapter from the top end of New London Road - the end nearest to the Rising Sun Public House. The houses on the same side nearer to Wood Street, for some reason are classified as being in Moulsham Street. I could never understand this as I thought Moulsham Street ended near the last set of Oaklands Park gates. However, to keep the record straight, I will work my way down New London Road from the Rising Sun. In my time the licensees were the Howitt family. I went to school with their son John who, later in life I understand committed suicide.

During the war as young lads, we went to the scene of aircraft crashes and found a number of unexploded bullets. I remember one day we found about two hundred near the scene of a crashed plane further down London Road - more about this later. We took the bullets into Oaklands Park and removed the bullet heads from the cases and then took out the Cordite, laying the pieces end to end. The area covered was about 25 yards into the bushes where the Sebastapol Cannon now stands. On a signal from John I lit the end of the Cordite and the ignition shot along the line at an alarming pace and ended up behind the shelter where the park workmen were taking a rest. This gave them and us a hell of a fright, as we never expected the flash to go so quickly. Needless to say we never tried this experiment again.

Just below the Rising Sun were two pairs of houses, where lived some of the gentry of the town. During the war my father, brother and I were returning from a fishing trip in the Recreation ground at about mid-day on a summer afternoon when we heard a terrific roar and coming down at a fast rate was a Spitfire which had been shot at by a German fighter plane and the pilot killed. It crashed into a pair of these houses and bullets went off at an alarming rate. We were first on the scene and my young brother went into the inferno with me to see if we could get the pilot out. Alas he was dead and we could do nothing for him. We got out fairly quickly as it was dangerous - my brother emerging with the thumb of the dead pilot which he had found in the wreckage. Later in life I learned that the pilot was a young Naval officer.

Soon a Captain Devlin who lived nearby came prancing up the road to take control of proceedings. Apparently he was a retired police officer and now in charge of the special constables. An arrogant man who had no time for young boys like my brother and myself.

Farleigh now the Chelmsford Hospice was the large house on the same side of the road. It was owned by Doctor Sir Ivor Beauchamp (Baronet). He was a very pleasant person and would often sponsor the various activities in which my mother was engaged in organising, whist drives or rummage sales either for the Vicarage Dilapidation fund or some other wartime activity.

Houses going down the road were occupied by various people. Phoenix House was the home of the Crompton Parkinson apprentices. Many a time I have been in there to organise a table tennis match against the apprentices team for Widford Youth Club. Sheila Mulvey ran the adjacent private school called Skansen, mainly for the very young.

The large building now occupied by BBC Essex, was called Fanum House and was the home of the Automobile Association. Across the Writtle Road was the home of a Mrs. Peake, who bred Cocker Spaniels; my parents brought one from her. This dog turned out to be rather snappy and did not last long in our household. This house has now been enlarged, and become South Lodge Hotel. The Borough Council Nursery School was the next main building. During the war I believe this was another British restaurant, where members of the public could obtain a very nourishing meal reasonably priced.

Moving down the road were a number of very large houses occupied by the gentry of the day. One was the home of Frederick Spalding the famous and well loved photographer. I do not remember Fred Spalding but his daughter

Winifred was a friend of my parents and I often visited this house. Winifred was a very good golfer and she played at what was then called Chelmsford Golf Links in Widford.

St. Philip's Priory Convent School came next. The only connection I had here was with my cousin Brenda Turrall who was a pupil. Brenda used to come to our house in Widford Road from school to await the arrival of her parents to take her home.

Next came the very large house owned by the then Mayor of Chelmsford Alderman J. Ockleford Thompson. The family were killed in the war when a German bomb caused a direct hit on their house known as Brierley Place, Alderman Thompson was a director of the Essex Chronicle.

St. Anne's Private School for small boys and girls came next. All the pupils had to wear the regulation clothes with grey short flannel trousers for boys and grey skirts for girls. Blue edged blazers, hats and caps were also worn - as they are today.

Between there and Anchor Street there were more houses occupied by the gentry. One of the houses beyond Anchor Street was where my father stayed when he first came to Chelmsford. It was owned by the Reeman family and they were great friends of my parents.

The Roman Catholic Church was the next main building. I do remember the priest was the Very Reverend Canon Michael Wilson. A very friendly man who always had a word for you if you met him in the street.

Behind the grey walls further down from the Catholic Church and hidden by very large trees was the Chelmsford Club. To me this was a mystery building and one which needed exploring. On a number of occasions I climbed the wall to see what was going on inside. All I found was smartly dressed men with large cars smoking cigars as they left the building.

Later in life I found that this was an exclusive men's club where lunches were served, snooker and other games played and usually the people

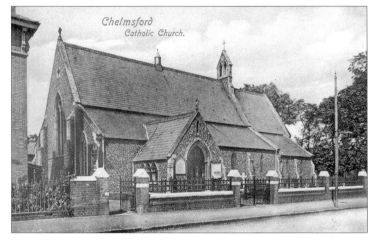

Chelmsford Catholic Church.

attending were from the business fraternity in Chelmsford. George Barford the Town Clerk and my previous employer was one of the members. I think it is still an exclusive men's club.

Across New Writtle Street was the annexe to the Chelmsford and Essex Hospital known as Bellfield. It appeared this was a rest home for those just out of hospital. Later it was turned into a residence for the hospital nurses. Surgeon Harry Platts had his residence alongside.

The large hospital building with its imposing front, took in patients from Chelmsford and its surrounds. Fortunately I only had to stay in this place once after I broke my arm playing football at the age of sixteen. This was operated on by the fearsome surgeon H.A.H. Harris who also lived in New London Road.

When I went back after some eight weeks for him to examine my arm, the plaster was cut off by a nurse with a pair of shears. Halfway through she cut into my arm and the plaster filled with blood. I have the scar to this day.

When Mr. Harris saw my arm and the X-ray he said it was set wrong and promptly broke the joint in front of me without any anaesthetic. I nearly died on the spot. It took another six weeks for the bones to heal and it is still not the same as it was before the accident.

Adjacent to the hospital was the strict Baptist Chapel. It was here that my Governess Daisy Rolph, worshipped on

INFIRMARY, NEW LONDON Rd. CHELMSFORD.

a Sunday. Surgeons and physicians Cummins and Corner owned the houses along the road.

Parkway that awful bisecting road did not exist in those days. A few small houses stood between the Chapel and the Rural District Council Offices which is now an Insurance Office. My contact with this place was through a number of people - Mr. H. Gowers and Mr. Menhinick from Roxwell, and the clerk, Mr. Cecil Plumtree, who I often met when working for Chelmsford Borough Council. An employee and old school friend was Wesley Holden who worked in the Treasurers Department. Wes was later transferred to Chelmsford Borough Council when the amalgamation in 1974 took place with the RDC. He is now retired devoting most of his time to the Salvation Army where he is their treasurer.

L.M. Linn insurance brokers occupied the next building. My parents arranged their house insurance with this firm. Jack Linn lived in Links Drive. He was a keen golfer and also a supporter of the Chelmsford Amateur Operatic Society. There followed R.H. Trump the hairdresser and Wisbeys the builders and next was the Thistle Guest House and tea rooms.

Various offices were along the way before the very large and imposing building known as the Institute, housing the first church of Christ Scientist. The frontage of the Institute still stands behind which are various offices.

After the iron bridge over the River Can came the surgery run by the effervescent Dr. J.T. Whitley, a favourite doctor of many Chelmsford people. Fred Kearsley had his dental practice alongside. For many years he was a Borough Councillor. Next door were a number of offices including those of accountants Mayor, Cuttle and Co before they moved further up New London Road. The Co-op Bank was the next building. I opened my first account here and I was one of its early customers. One of the clerks at this bank was Roger Le'Strange who was the leader of the Widford Youth Club.

I always remember this bank as one of the assistants who thought he was the cats whiskers, came up to me when I went in for some money and said in a loud voice. "Your account is overdrawn by 30/- and you can't have any money". That afternoon my salary cheque was due to be paid in. I never forgot this incident and almost changed my account, however after 52 years I am still with the Co-op Bank who have now moved their premises to Market Road.

Solicitors Hill and Abbott followed, then Coote and Warren's coal offices, Bayes the old style provision merchant, Mrs. Davies the furrier and Thorn the ladies' hairdresser. The Chelmsford Boys' Club was behind the offices which have since been pulled down. They used to collect waste paper for the war effort. Bolingbrokes had their dressmaking department here following the fire at their main premises across the road in 1948. My wife worked there for some time before she left and went to Marconi's.

A.F. White the estate agent had a place along there where I often went and paid my aunt's rent. Miss Godfrey had her little shop selling children's outfits which was adjacent to the Little Tindal Cafe. Then came Dace's music shop where a wonderful young assistant, Peter Andrews was employed. Peter later moved to the Weekly News for whom he still does occasional reporting even though now "retired". Mr. Bush a local organist and piano tutor also worked there. Then came Miss Turners, wet fish shop and fruit shop, then Stockwell another ladies' hairdresser before we came to Wainwright's Café on the corner.

Across London Road at the lower end, was the wholesale department of Luckin-Smiths later taken over by Buttons. Smaller shops were adjacent owned variously by carpet or clothing firms, before we came to a small hairdressers' shop set back from the road which was run by Perkins. Many a time have I had my hair cut at this establishment.

Bolingbroke's rear entrance was next before the main shop of Wenley's the house furnisher. The two firms have now amalgamated. Captain Wenley was a regular worshipper at Widford Church and in later years he was very much involved with the St. John Ambulance Brigade.

The area along here was like an arcade and housed various small shops including Percy Uttin the tailor, Edna Duffield florist, Keens the opticians, the inland Revenue offices, Daniel the jeweller and Dunkley's pianos and piano tuners; next came Woodwards, the typewriter company from Ipswich. This firm had some connection with my family as my cousin Violet Turrall married the owner. The manager of this shop whose name was Sid Fieldus used to play football for Ipswich and Chelmsford.

Across the river stood the London Road Congregational Church, long since gone, which had a very strong Boys' Brigade and a number of my pals belonged to this.

A number of small offices followed and then came CLESCO the County of London Electric Supply Company, who controlled our electricity in those days, this is where we went to pay our electric light bills. Adjacent was a little sweet shop known as Sunset owned by a Herbert Bradley. Many a time during the war Herbert found some cigarettes for my parents or a few extra sweets. Essex Electric Installation run by Mr. Negus was next. Mr. Negus had an enormous moustache and ran the company with a colleague Eddie Edwards, with whom in later life I had a lot of business dealings, especially with air conditioning units in outside broadcast vehicles for Marconi. Further along the road were the Labour Party headquarters, William Smith Magnetos and the Chelmsford Provident Society before reaching Friars Place.

On the next corner was the Congregational Church Sunday school and then J.B. Slythe Monumental Masons. They had all their gravestones and other statues displayed in a yard adjacent to the road. Windley Brothers the engineers were adjacent and these premises were at one time the Chelmsford Skating Rink. In fact some of the work done by Marconi's during the war was at this place.

Youngs the Coach Builders had their offices and garage adjacent followed by Eastern Automobiles garage run by one John Cox, with whom in my youth I was acquainted. He eventually married Betty Bragg from the Widford Café.

Between here and the Red Lion Public House were mainly private houses. At the top end next to Luckin the funeral furnisher, was the cemetery for non-conformists and then the residence of Surgeon, Melville Sheppard. He was a very well known and well liked surgeon and wards have been named after him in the local hospitals.

Other well known local people who lived in this part of the road were Mr. Harris, Surgeon, Mr. Illife dentist, Albert Cutts of Green the optician and Tom Windibank one of the directors of the local industrial firm Crompton Parkinson.

Chapter Nine

# INDUSTRIAL CHELMSFORD

In my youth it seemed that all the men worked at the main factories of the town, Crompton's, Hoffman, Marconi's or Christy's. The town was known for its industries, and thousands of people worked in them. It is a far cry now from those days, with modern equipment taking the workload of many people so that the work force has been drastically lowered and all the main factories are in demise except Marconi's.

Crompton's (or Crompton Parkinson its official name) was situated in Writtle Road opposite the Borough cemetery. It was established by Colonel Crompton and although its original site was in Anchor Street, the factory moved to Writtle Road during the early 1900's employing several thousand people in the manufacture of street lighting equipment, generators and instruments.

At lunch times and in the evening, crowds of employees would leave the factory on their bicycles or queue up to catch buses home, the men nearly always wearing cloth caps and smoking cigarettes as it was not allowed during working hours in the actual factory.

Crompton's had a wonderful social centre just inside Writtle Road near the railway bridge. This place also acted as a canteen for the Crompton workers and staff. It also had a wonderful dance floor and hosted many dances and other forms of entertainment particularly during the war when concerts and talent shows were staged.

Before this social centre was built, the Bertram Mills circus used this site for their annual shows. Many a time I visited this circus with my parents. It was really first class entertainment.

All the factories had hooters which sounded at various times during the day either to call people to work or advise them of leaving off time. Each factory had a distinct sound on its hooter and to avoid congestion, times were staggered for start and finish of work for the day.

Marconi's or to give it the official name, Marconi's Wireless Telegraph Company, started off in business in the town in 1898 at a small warehouse previously used as a silk factory on the corner of Hall Street and Mildmay Road. This was the world's first wireless factory employing 26 men and boys. Young lads from the age of 12 were able to get jobs even though their tasks were mundane such as floor sweeping or making tea.

Two enormous masts were erected for wireless experiments, but these were removed when the factory relocated to New Street.

In 1916 the factory moved to New Street where it still stands although extensively altered from its original design. Manufacture here was of wireless sets, Morse transmitting equipment and later broadcast and television transmitters and television cameras, HF transmitters, mobile radio, radar, marine equipment, satellite transmitters and many other similar items.

Marconi's was probably the largest factory in the area and although originally the headquarters of the company, it is now only a satellite unit of the parent company Marconi plc whose headquarters have moved to Coventry.

The factory in New Street is situated near the small railway bridge and opposite the railway goods yard. The bridge, originally designed for horse and cart, was so low that only single decker buses could get through taking up all the road as they passed. These and of course the many cyclists, had to cope with animals being driven from the goods yard to the cattle market in Market Road. Real problems existed until the late 1950's when the bridge size was increased and the road widened to take two lines of traffic and double decker buses.

The road adjacent to the factory was named after the company and quite a number of employees lived there. Most people travelled to work by bus, bicycle or Shanks pony. Not many people could afford cars.

Chelmsford factories were the target for German bombers during the 1939-45 war as they were making equipment to assist the British Army, Navy and Air Force in their fight against the Nazi power. Both Marconi's and Hoffmans were bombed and there were many casualties. After the war the British Army captured a German Air Force Base and found a scale model of the main Marconi and Hoffman factory showing the railway line and adjacent houses. Even the camouflage which Marconi put on their buildings were detailed on this model. This model is now housed with other Marconi archives.

Hoffman or to give it the correct name the Hoffman Roller Bearing Manufacturing Company was situated at the corner of New Street and Rectory Lane and occupied a very large site. Here they manufactured ball and roller bearings which were used in every conceivable mode of transport or machinery. Leather belt driven lathes and cutting tools were visible through windows from the road and at one time the factory employed 15,000 people. In later years the company was taken over by RHP (Ransom Hoffman Pollard) and in the early 1970's all production ceased and many employees were made redundant.

Christy Brothers and Christy & Norris had their factory on the main Broomfield Road, one Company made electrical goods whilst the other produced more mechanical items such as machinery for mills and agricultural requirements.

Before ownership of wireless sets became popular, many Chelmsford houses were equipped with what was called a relay service. Christy's provided this by a small box with loudspeaker and tuning control fed directly from an overhead wire system. The relay equipment of the various programmes was housed in the main factory area in Broomfield Road. Alas this service is no more, the factory has been pulled down and now a private housing development occupies the site.

EEV Waterhouse Lane was an infant company in the 1940's born from the old valve division of Marconi. It celebrated its 50th year in 1997 and now occupies a large area of Waterhouse Lane producing some of the finest electronic equipment required in this modern age. The original building known as Waterhouse Farm is the main dining area for senior officials of the Company. This is a lovely 14th century design with many oak beams and wall panels. Conferences and discussions also take place in this building.

Marconi's Works, Chelmsford. Front View.

Chapter Ten

# THE RECREATION GROUND

The "Rec" as it was referred to, was the area in Chelmsford which in spring and summer was the place to rest and relax by the river or the lake.

The River Can flowed gently through this lovely park and near the railway was a large lake full of fish which many a time with my father and brother I have visited and fished.

Entrances were either over the concrete bridge in Seymour Street next to the Falcon Bowling Club, at the side of the viaducts adjacent to Burgess Well Road, down the side of Park Road or over the rickety bridge which was accessed through London Road and alongside Wisbey the builders yard. There was also another entrance at the bottom of Threadneedle Street.

*Recreation Grounds, Chelmsford*

*On the Cann, Chelmsford*

The park was laid out with beautiful flower gardens, trees and a band pavilion with an adjacent café. Also in the garden were two rather large 1914-18 war guns on wheels.

On carnival day the whole area became the scene of a Fun day for parents and children with many side-shows, a fair and displays by local dance groups.

Beneath the viaducts were a number of grass tennis courts with a bowling green alongside. On match days access to the Chelmsford City Football Ground was by a special iron bridge over the river Can.

Many a time in the cold winter months I have skated on the lake. The ice one winter (I think in 1939), was said to be twelve inches thick and in fact I remember seeing a tractor on the ice. It was alleged that in the lake was a locomotive which during the 1920's ran off the rails and down the embankment into the lake. I have not been able to establish this fact but I was told that during the dredging and building of the lake many years ago one of the steam driven diggers fell into the lake and was not recovered. Perhaps one day the true story will be told.

The river running through the park was used extensively by rowing boats. These were hired from the back of the Queens Head Public House which was situated opposite Woolworths in the High Street. During Carnival Week these boats were illuminated with lanterns and in the evening were a lovely sight as they went up and down the river.

Although I was never a witness to any incident, this part of the river was a place where a number of suicides took place. I can remember my parents relating such incidents.

The river itself was also good for fishing and many a net full of good roach were taken from the stretch within the park.

Flooding frequently took place when the river overflowed due to the heavy rains, and vast areas were completely covered in water. On the odd occasion fish from the river could be found in small pools once the floods had subsided.

During the Second World War the Recreation Ground was closed as the area was equipped with rocket guns to

Chelmsford.                                    The Bandstand, Recreation Grounds.

protect the town. I believe these were manned partly by the regular Army and partly by the local Home Guard.

# Chapter Eleven

# VICTORIA ROAD

Starting at the railway station end, the house on the corner, partly in Duke Street, was the surgery of a dentist, named Russell. A little further down the road were Pooles the bookbinders, a specialist firm where many of the Borough Council minute books were made. I only remember two people in this place. One was the owner Mr. Poole who was a very kind man the other was his son Ron. In later life I met Ron at the Regent Theatre when the Chelmsford Amateur Operatic Society were putting on their shows. Ron was a scene shifter, doing this in his spare time.

Later on Ron led the carnival procession in his car announcing as he went along from his microphone and loudspeaker system. I think Ron married one of the carnival queens.

Adjacent to Pooles was the YWCA. Obviously out of bounds to the boys but on many occasions we attended parties and dances at this place. Along the road were a number of houses and I think a coal merchants before the local offices of Driver and Ling, scrap metal merchants.

There were more houses opposite near New Street where the police station now stands then came the Chelmsford model laundry. Between here and the Bradbridge Mill, now the Riverside Inn, were more terraced houses. On the corner of Victoria Road was the E.R.C.B offices (Essex River Catchment Board), now Rivers House.

Coming back towards the station from the Springfield Road end and on the opposite side, were various houses and small shops and the auction rooms of Cooper Hirst. On the other side of the river Chelmer was the area destined for the new cattle market which was moved from Market Road in later years.

Where the Post Office buildings now stand was a street of small houses called Regina Road, followed by many small cottages, until on the corner of New Street the old Cathedral Girls' School building which was later used as the Marconi Social Club where dances and other indoor events were held on a regular basis.

Across the road leading towards the station were a few more houses and behind them Andrews, funeral furnishers garages and mortuary. Here was Turner the mens' hairdressers, Jewell the ladies' hairdresser, Denham and Archer fruiterers and then the YMCA (Young Mens Christian Association). Many a time have I attended this place as a young man for games, talks and food. Mr. Peters was the warden in charge. He was a very likeable character. The next main building was County Motor Works and on the corner of Duke Street was Hawke's sweet shop.

Adjacent to the railway station under the viaducts were a number of lock up premises occupied by various organisations. One was for fruit and vegetables another a coal merchant's and one for a paper delivery company. Taxi cabs and Carter Paterson delivery vehicles lined the station approaches. Thomas Moy the local coal merchant also had a small office in the station yard run by a Mr. Empson.

# Chapter Twelve

# CHELMSFORD CHARACTERS

During the last 50 years there have been a number of Chelmsford "characters". I do not know a lot about them but those I remember and the stories often heard about them are related here.

## Bundles

He was a man who often walked through the streets of Chelmsford dressed mainly in a dirty black overcoat with a cap and carrying many "bundles" under his arm, hence his name.

"Bundles" frequented the centre of Chelmsford often asking for the odd cup of water or I suspect food from the various shops. Sometimes he was seen on the outskirts of the town, often sleeping under a hedge.

Commonly known as a tramp, "Bundles" I understand once occupied a room at the old workhouse which was at that time part of the St. John's Hospital complex, and known as "The Union". Part of this workhouse still exists in Wood Street.

The story goes that "Bundles" was once engaged to a Miss Carter of Gt. Baddow and was crossed in love. He decided to live the life of a tramp following this upset in his romantic life. He died a tramp even though it was thought he came from a good background and his family were quite wealthy.

A number of people referred to him as "Moses" but I never discovered the reason for this.

## Miller

He lived in a little cottage next to the fire station in Waterhouse Lane. A very strange man he walked around with a plastic bag on his head and wore very scruffy clothes. He even had a strange receptacle under his nose to collect his "dew drops".

Miller was always first at the library in Duke Street and into the reading room to read the Financial Times. It was alleged he studied the paper for stocks and shares.

When he died he left over £130,000 but lived the life of a hermit.

## May Say

I have, in detailing the occupants of New Street, mentioned May Say. She was a well endowed lady who had an awesome vocabulary of swear words. No matter who you were, she would shout some abuse as you walked by her little hut in New Street which she called her home. It was more like a beach hut or summerhouse but was always decorated and in a little garden at the side she grew many plants and vegetables, it was also decorated with stones and shells.

Her only job as far as I knew, was as a cleaner in the then Vestry Hall opposite to where her little hut stood. The Crown Court and solicitors offices now occupy the site where she lived.

## Bob Bailey

A dear old paper boy, Bob always sat on a window ledge of the Corn Exchange to sell his evening papers. Not very well educated, Bob's only job was in the newspaper trade and he had a cheery smile and a very red face, no doubt brought about by the odd nip of whisky from one of the local pubs in Tindal Street. He was very reliable and always had the papers ready for me to deliver to County Hall after school. He walked at "quarter to three" and I suspect he had very bad feet. He always wore a brown trilby hat.

## Flacky

He was the man who sold the Evening News from his three wheeler tricycle which I suspect he obtained at some time from the Walls Ice Cream people. He always wore a grey trilby hat and in addition to selling newspapers from the area around the Corn Exchange, he delivered some on his way home to the Boarded Barns Estate.

## Jimmy

A very small man, he was another tramp but sold newspapers outside the Regent Theatre. He wore a cloth cap and trousers too long for him which were hoisted up at the knees by pieces of string. He sold the Star and Evening Standard and had no fixed abode.

He always had a runny nose which he wiped on his sleeve. His part time job was to operate the potato peeling machine at Sid Rowe's Fish and Chip shop in Springfield Road.

## Len Gifford

A very tall and erect gentleman, Len was employed by the Chelmsford Borough Council as the market tolls collector. He was an ex-Indian Army soldier and served in many campaigns. Len always had the job as mace bearer to the Mayor of the town and looked splendid dressed in his blue uniform with white trimmings and tricorn hat.

Len was a favourite with the market traders and they always made sure that he was well looked after, particularly at the festive season.

## "Peaso" Hammond

Peaso as he was known had a horse and cart and was what we might call "an odd job man". It appeared his main occupation was to sell vegetables from his cart. In the summer season you could hear him call out as he trundled up the road "Peaso". He had collected pounds of peas ready to sell to the housewives in his area - hence his name.

In addition to this, which appeared to be his regular job, he often carted furniture for a small fee from auction sales or other shops in the town.

He was always at the poultry market on a Friday holding up the chickens, geese, ducks, rabbits and anything else for the auctioneer whilst bidding took place. He would even deliver the items for a small sum of money.

## Runcorn

I never knew his christian name, he was the Caretaker at County Hall in the old King Edward Avenue entrance. He had a flat at the top of the building for his family.

An ex military man he had been an RSM and was very tall and erect. His claim to be one of my characters was that he was a Kings Yeoman of the Guard and was often called to ceremonial duties in London. He looked very resplendent in his uniform although I only saw photographs of him all dressed up as he obviously went to London in "civvies".

He was very strict and had a gruff voice. Many times he chastised me when, as a boy, I delivered evening newspapers to the staff in County Hall.

Chapter Thirteen

# EVENTS

People tend to forget the events and celebrations which went on in and around Chelmsford. I recall some of them here.

## The Chelmsford Carnival

This was and still is held on the first Saturday in July. It depended on the number of floats anticipated as to where the procession started but I remember it traversed Duke Street, High Street, Moulsham Street and into New London Road ending up in what we called the Recreation ground or "Rec" (but now has the posh name of Central Park).

The main feature of the carnival was the stop outside the Chelmsford and Essex Hospital in New London Road where as many patients as possible were wheeled on their beds into the forecourt to see the procession. All money collected went to this hospital.

The procession was headed by "John Bull" who used to be a symbol of Britain, a bluff, robust fellow, with a Union Jack waistcoat. This part was played by a Mr. Fewell who for many years was the owner of a milk firm in the town. The number of floats was far greater than we get today, the highlights being those entered by the big firms in the town, Cromptons, Hoffmans, Marconi's and Christy's. Usually the apprentices of these famous companies were given the task of coming up with a theme for the floats. They were magnificent and evoked friendly rivalry between the firms.

The evening in the "Rec" was always great fun with a fair, high wire acts and of course the firework displays and boats on the river. People really enjoyed themselves and whole families treated this as the highlight of the year. Alas although the event is still carried out, enthusiasm is not so strong for either the procession or the event in the evening which is currently held in Admirals Park.

## Annual Sports Days

These turned out to be more like gala days and were held by Marconi's in Waterhouse Lane, Hoffmans at St. Fabian's Drive and Crompton's at Wood Street on their sports fields.

These companies competed against each other in some of the events although most were for employees of each firm. There were some very fine athletes in all the three companies and a lot of these people went on to compete for Essex in their particular events.

It was always a family day out and hundreds of people enjoyed not only the athletics but also the many side-shows which went on alongside. Alas these events no longer take place and some of the sports grounds are now housing estates or superstores as the companies have gone out of business. The only sports field left is that of Marconi's which is now in Beehive Lane.

## The Circus

Bertram Mills or Billy Smarts Circus often visited Chelmsford. The main site for the former was in Writtle Road where later stood the Crompton Social Club. The Kings Head Meadow accessed adjacent to the old Odeon Cinema was generally the site for Billy Smarts Circus.

The Circus always created a lot of attention as in those days the acts were mainly with animals although clowns and high wire events were also prominent.

Local advertising took place and on the odd occasion animals especially the elephants were paraded through the town. This gave young boys the opportunity of walking with the animals back to the Circus tent and either getting a free ticket or ensuring they were able to help the ringmaster or the keeper feed the animals.

## The Bands

Most weekends the bandstand in the Recreation Ground was occupied either by a local brass or silver band or by an invited military band.

Sunday afternoons in particular, crowds would sit in the park with their children listening to the bandsmen who gave them a good selection of music - rousing, happy, tranquil or sad. I remember on one occasion a German band was playing in the park just before the second world war and my father told me the story of some young boys sucking a lemon in front of the man playing the Euphonium in an attempt to put him off playing the correct notes. Apparently it worked.

Other bands often marched through the town on various occasions. The Salvation Army, especially on a Sunday marched to the Shire Hall with their banners flying and gathered the crowds for a service which was usually well attended.

Boy Scouts with their trumpets and the local Boys Brigade were often seen marching through the town on their way to a camp or church parade.

Chapter Fourteen

# UNUSUAL HAPPENINGS

Many incidents always occur in one's life. Some funny, some sad, some interesting and others well????

Here I relate some I remember.

At Marconi's I was Captain of a divisional cricket team known as "Springbows". The team was mainly made up of people in the Installation Drawing Office of which I was a member.

We were a very strong team and swept the board in the Chelmsford Evening League winning the league and cup on several occasions. We played against teams from the Railway, Hoffmans, Eastern National, Writtle, Cromptons, Christys, Chelmsford Borough Council and many others.

One evening we were playing Writtle on the village green. Going into bat first I hit the ball all over the ground and one massive six I put straight through the window of Greens the butchers. Obviously they were insured and I did apologise to the owner after the match.

Two weeks later we were again at Writtle and somehow the butcher had heard that my team were playing. The butcher, although his shop was closed, decided to take no chances and sat all evening outside his shop wearing his butchers apron and straw hat. I did not repeat the incident but did hit a number of sixes very close to the butchers shop.

My prowess as a big hitter was also demonstrated at the small Admirals Park pitch. I often hit sixes into the road and into the water tower in the adjacent Tower Gardens; sometimes the ball was lost.

The lower pitch of Admirals Park gave me the opportunity of hitting the ball into the adjacent River Can for small boys to earn a "tanner" to retrieve the ball (a "tanner" was the old sixpenny piece, now out of currency).

Another incident comes to mind and that was an episode of bird nesting. Adjacent to our house in Widford Road was an area with trees and grass which was known as "The Plantation". One day in early spring my brother Michael told me of a birds' nest some fifty feet up one of the Sycamore trees. We both climbed to about twenty feet when he decided he could not go any further. I decided to go up to the nest and found it was a tree sparrow's with something like six eggs in the nest. I took two and put them in my mouth and started to come down. At that point the branch gave way and I came crashing down. Apparently I stopped momentarily on the same branch on which my brother was watching before crashing to the ground absolutely winded. Down came my brother very worried in case I had broken my limbs. All I got was a little bruising. "Where are the eggs?" he said. "In my mouth" I replied after some time. Even after the fall and being winded the eggs were still whole.

During the war years we, like many other families, did our best to help the war effort by having garden stalls to raise money for the many requirements. Either warships, aeroplanes or Red Cross activities. We sold our toys and other items in an effort to raise money. We received very nice thank you letters from well known people. At the same time we gave up many of our treasured toys. Some of which were given reluctantly.

Chapter Fifteen

# THE FOOTBALL AND CRICKET CLUB

## Chelmsford City Football Club

My early recollections of Chelmsford City Football Club are of times just before the second world war. My father was a regular supporter of the club and took us to each home match for either the first team or the reserves. We went to the ground in New Writtle Street in the car of an opposite neighbour, a Mr. Wilson who also brought his son Armistice in the little red and black Singer Saloon.

In pre-war days, Chelmsford City Football Club was a team to be reckoned with and had some excellent players. I remember sitting on the wall on the "barn" side or on a box and watching the team. They had a great run in the FA Cup just before the war beating many really good teams including Portsmouth and got to the fifth round losing eventually to Birmingham away from home.

Difficult to remember the 1938-39 team but some of the players were Dollman in goal, Sliman the Captain, Ben Burley outside right, Bill Parry wing half, Len Jones outside left and Palethorpe inside forward.

After the war a number of local lads played for the City when they were in the Southern League. They often won the league and cup with these lads amongst whom were, Denny Foreman centre forward, Buddy Gowers outside right, Ben Marden outside left (who eventually went to Arsenal), Reg Folkard wing half, Jake Farley centre half, Eric Turner goalkeeper, Eric Childs goalkeeper, and Derek Tiffin centre half. Other well known people who played for the club were Frank Soo, Fred and Len Jones, Dick Goulden, Charley Hurst, Geoff Hurst who went on to play for West Ham and England and was the hero of the 1966 World Cup scoring three goals.

A regular amusing feature of these matches was the half time announcement by the Chairman of the Board of Directors. It started with a roar over the loudspeakers and the words "Alderman Langton here". This was the signal for a lot of booing and shouting whilst the Chairman tried to make his speech. He was a very short man who wore a homberg and sported a waistcoat pocket watch and chain over a rather large corporation. He lived in Galleywood. His son was also a director of the Club.

Harry Warren was probably the first and most successful manager. Unfortunately the club has not gained the football league status which some of their old opponents have achieved. Support for the Club has been very fickle.

## Chelmsford Cricket Club

The Essex County Cricket ground in New Writtle Street was the home of the Chelmsford Cricket Club before the County moved in. Previously the club played on the ground where Marconi Mobile now stands in New Street. The club in those days was called the Chelmsford Church Institute and the ground was rented from the Church Commissioners. Apparently when Marconi's wanted to build on the Clubs cricket ground, they had to buy the ground for the Club in New Writtle Street which was nothing more than a field.

My father often told the story of how he with his brothers and friends helped to shape the ground behind the Chelmsford and Essex Hospital. A long Hawthorn hedge ran from the hospital right down to the river and he helped remove this. It was many years before the ground took shape and is now one of the finest grounds in the country.

My cricket career really started at school but, my father was a county umpire and he encouraged me to play on decent cricket pitches. I joined Great Baddow Cricket Club playing on the Baddow "Rec" for a number of years before joining Brentwood Cricket Club where my father was the regular umpire.

It was very difficult to get into the first team as they had so many good players. I did however command a regular second team place either as a wicket keeper or as a fielder and opening bat.

I remember particularly well one incident at this ground. We were playing Chelmsford and they had sent a very strong team. We fielded first and I was very deep long on when in came to bat, Bill Bradley. Bradley was a schoolmaster at Moulsham School where he gave me a hard time. He was the PT and Games Master. It would appear at some time my father had given him out at a cricket match and he was not pleased. When I went to the school he went out of his way to eliminate me from the school football and cricket teams. He never gave me a reason but I think he was jealous of the sporting prowess of the Turrall family which had produced many county players at football, hockey, cricket, bowls and boxing as well as athletics.

Returning to the cricket incident, Bradley had hit two fours off the bowling and went for a big six hit off the next ball. I saw this coming and ran fully thirty yards and caught the ball one handed before it crossed the boundary. Bradley was furious, even more so when he saw it was me.

The time came for Brentwood to bat and eventually when I went in, Bradley as Captain, decided to bowl. He wasn't a fast bowler but was able to spin the ball. After a steady start I decided to have a go and I knocked him all over the ground, much to the delight of my Uncle Walter who, although deaf and dumb was himself a good cricketer and had to come to watch. I think I scored 34 and eventually Brentwood won. I got some of my own back but was never able to repeat the incident as Bradley, obviously older than me, retired to be an umpire.

Eventually I returned to Chelmsford and played regularly for the second eleven as by that time my father was umpire for the club. Unfortunately I did not get the opportunity of playing county cricket but I did play on many good county grounds.

# Chapter Sixteen

# OTHER SPORTS

Apart from football and cricket which are mentioned in other chapters, Chelmsford the County Town of Essex, boasted activities in many other sports.

## Rugby

Not in the national class in this sport, the Chelmsford Rugby Club however were quite strong in the Eastern Counties. They still have their headquarters at Coronation Park in the Springfield area of the town.

Names who conjure up memories during the late 1940's were the Gunns, Gammies and Bellamys. I seem to remember Ted Barford the son of the then Town Clerk also played rugby for Chelmsford after his return from the war.

Rugby was not a sport played by the factories and the opposition for the Rugby Club came from other towns in the Essex or London area.

## Table Tennis

Many teams took part in the local league and among them the main factory teams of Hoffmans, Cromptons and Marconi's. Other teams were Abbey Works, ECC, Chelmsford and Great Baddow. I even ran a Widford Youth Club Team in the lower divisions of the league.

On Finals Night it was always a pleasure to watch the local talent. One person I will always remember was Charlie Wheeler. He worked and played for Marconi's and he was a very talented player particularly on defence. Many people tried and failed to beat him. The size of his bat was enough to put off would be pretenders to his singles crown. It was almost the size of a frying pan. For many years Charlie won the Chelmsford singles title and represented the local league in inter-league matches.

Another was Tom Mayer. He ended up as the Managing Director of Marconi Communications. He was a good player and chairman of the local league for many years. Bill Lang was the Secretary of the Marconi table tennis team and he was also a very formidable player together with another, Tony Condon.

Eileen Ainsworth, (now Mrs. Eileen Hance) was a member of the Chelmsford team who had their headquarters in the cricket pavilion in New Writtle Street.

Table tennis was played in many different halls. Cromptons played either in the cricket pavilion in Wood Street or in the social club in Writtle Road. Hoffmans played in the lovely dance hall in New Street whilst Marconi's played in the Canteen in New Street. Abbey Works used their canteen in Cottage Place behind the Cathedral. Alas this is no longer there.

## Hockey

The main team in the area was Chelmsford who played on the county cricket ground in New Writtle Street. Nowadays they play on the Chelmer Park in Beehive Lane. Although there was no "league" there was inter-club rivalry between the works teams of Cromptons, Hoffmans and Marconi's. Sometimes it was all men or all ladies teams. Other times it was mixed teams. Many a good player for the county has come from these local sides.

The Essex County Council boasted several hockey teams and they with Writtle College and other local sides competed with the cream of the area. One player from the Essex County Council team was a member of their side into his sixties. He even at times turned out for the ECC football team. He was good at both sports and many people will remember the name of Harold Parkins.

## Bowls

Here again apart from the Chelmsford Clubs of Falcon, Princess Marie Louise and Chelmsford itself, there was friendly rivalry from the factory teams of Hoffman, Crompton and Marconi's who each had excellent club rinks and facilities. Again many of the players represented the county from the locality. One player comes to mind from Marconi's - Sid Fagg a member of the well known Kent county cricket family. Sid was an excellent bowler and won many local championships.

Other teams in the area were, Little Baddow, Seabrooks of Boreham, Estric, Stock and Writtle.

In those days the factory teams even employed permanent ground staff to ensure their greens were kept in tip-top condition. Names like Creasy of Marconi's and Sid Cooper of Cromptons come to mind.

Chapter Seventeen

# FLOODS

Chelmsford was for ever being flooded when heavy rains swelled the two rivers, Chelmer and Can. Many times I have been in the High Street before it was made a pedestrian way, when the tar covered wooden blocks which formed the road were lifted as the flood water poured over them.

The Council workmen very rarely replaced them and many people took handcarts or wheelbarrows to collect those discarded. They made excellent firewood as the tar on them burned away. In those days everybody had open fires and once the coals and blocks started to burn the town in winter, was covered with smog.

Shops in the vicinity of the rivers were constantly being flooded and the fire brigade was kept very busy pumping water out of the cellars in which either coal or stock was kept.

Some of the worst floods were in the area of Moulsham Street and the Friars. They were nearest to where the rivers Can and Chelmer met, at a point behind Springfield Road where the old Empire Cinema stood and which is now occupied by "Argos" super store.

Often have I walked through the Friars with the water at least two feet deep. The water went into the "Rec" and covered the Chelmsford Cricket Ground and at the rear of the Chelmsford and Essex Hospital.

In 1958 returning from a day out to see my parents on holiday in Clacton, we ran into a terrible storm along the Colchester Remembrance Avenue. I managed to get to Witham before I was stopped by the police having gone through very deep flood water and damaged the distributor of my open topped Morris Minor car. We spent the night on a bed in Byfords furniture showroom. I was friendly with their son Alan. We had with us our two week old son. I managed to get some hot water from the Spread Eagle pub for his drink and as we had run out of nappies my vest was brought into good use.

Next day, which was a Saturday, I managed to get a new distributor and we set off for Chelmsford. The fields on this September morning were flooded, particularly at Rivenhall where I had to go through some very deep water, some of which came into the car.

When we got to Springfield Road we could see that everywhere was flooded and we were the last car that the police allowed into Chelmsford before they shut all entrance roads and called a flood emergency.

Travelling through deep water along Victoria Road we eventually got to Broomfield Road and then home. After a while I ventured into the town on my bicycle to collect essential food for the family and the two week old baby son.

Another flood a few years later saw the whole of the "Rec" under water. People living in Prykes Drive behind the current fire station, were completely flooded and had to be rescued by boats. I was one of the helpers at that time.

The Baddow Meads near the Chelmer Road bypass was another area prone to flooding. I have been to this part of the town and witnessed terrible floods when it was impossible to see where the river ran. Baddow Road was impassable until the Council made arrangements to divert the path of the river and make concrete walls in the area where it passed through the town. The Chelmer and Blackwater canal had a number of locks and careful opening of these was necessary to alleviate flooding in the town. The canal ended behind the timber yard of Brown and Sons in Springfield Road/Navigation Road where for many years timber was hauled up from Maldon by horse drawn barges. This area is now "Coates Quay" and is being developed further.

Chapter Eighteen

# THE PARKS AND THE MUSEUM

Chelmsford has been blessed with a number of parks. Already described in a previous chapter is the "Rec" or as it is currently known, Central Park.

Other parks were Lionmede in Springfield Road, Admirals Park in Rainsford Road, Oaklands Park in Moulsham Street and although no longer a park, the Kings Head Meadow where the car park now stands near the Gas Works in Springfield/Baddow Road area. For many years the Kings Head Meadow housed football pitches and the annual circus erected its big top here.

Lionmede in Springfield Road was not a large area but it housed some very good tennis courts and of course a bowling green which are still in use. Football was also played on the main grass area.

Admirals Park in Rainsford Road was alongside the river Can and often young boys including myself went down there with our fishing nets and jam jars to catch tiddlers. Cricket and football were played here and in the adjacent Tower Gardens tennis and bowls. It is in these gardens that the famous Conduit which stood in Chelmsford High Street now rests. With the pedestrianisation of the High Street, it is a pity that the Chelmsford Borough Council could not have returned it to its original place instead of away from the main area of the town where only a few people can see it.

Apart from the "Rec", Oaklands Park in Moulsham Street has always been the most frequently visited. The main reason for this is because there are some fine grass and hard tennis courts, a football pitch and in days gone by a putting green in front of the Museum.

The Museum has been there for many years and in my younger days housed mainly stuffed animals and birds. A lot of the animals were donated by a Doctor Salter who carried out a number of expeditions in Russia and elsewhere shooting animals and having them stuffed and brought back to the museum. One feature for many years was a large white Polar Bear in a glass case and two fighting Bengal Tigers.

Oaklands Park was a good playground for us younger boys. The Sebastapol Cannon was there and this was the delight of boys clambering on it. Also it was a good hunting ground for birds nests.

The hard tennis courts were excellent and our son learned to play on these by having professional coaching lessons. Unfortunately he did not take up the game seriously.

Many a good game of football was played on the field at the rear of the museum, particularly in out of term

time or after school had finished for the day. A lot of good footballing careers started here. Some I remember are the Baldwin boys, Tich Dowsett, Reg Folkard and the Mann brothers.

# Chapter Nineteen

# THE FREEDOM OF THE BOROUGH

The freedom of the Borough of Chelmsford was only given on rare occasions. One such was to General Anderson of the United States Air Force whose forces were stationed at Weathersfield. The Chelmsford Borough Council decided because of the support given by the Americans in the war that this great honour should befall him.

At that time I was with the Borough Council and part of the procedure was to walk from the Council offices at the top end of Duke Street to the Shire Hall at the top end of the High Street in procession with the Mayor, Council officials and members of the Council all in their robes. A special oak casket containing the charter was made and I was given the task of heading the procession carrying this casket. For the occasion my parents bought me a black jacket, striped trousers and a black and white tie. They were very proud as I walked nervously carrying this box followed by a band playing and men of the Essex Regiment behind.

The General resplendent in uniform accepted the casket from the Mayor and the charter was read out by Town Clerk George Barford. A day I will never forget.

# Chapter Twenty

# MY HOME VILLAGE - WIDFORD

From the age of five years I lived in the village of Widford on the outskirts of Chelmsford. My parents moved here in 1935 having previously lived in Hill Road, Chelmsford.

My first real school was that in the village of Widford situated at the rear of St. Mary's Church. The school comprised as far as I remember two main classes for infants and juniors from the age of five up to the age of eleven. Miss Winifred Rankin was the Headmistress and Miss Wright took the senior of two classes, the other being run by a Miss Minnie Knight.

I never got to Miss Wright's class as I stayed with Minnie Knight for three years before going on to the brand new Moulsham School at the age of eight, although I remember having one or two terms at the Friars School just before going to Moulsham School.

The basics of reading, writing and arithmetic were taught and I enjoyed all of these. I had difficulty with division sums but after this was sorted I went on like a house on fire and in later life I became very good at maths. Spelling and the times table were drilled into us, as is often said "parrot fashion". It held me in good stead as mental arithmetic was one of my favourite pastimes. Today the calculator takes all the fun away from those learning maths.

One of the highlights of Widford School was the opportunity to play football on the adjacent playing field at break times and after school. Another was to listen to the school band. It was run by the top class and one song I remember was "Fire in the Valley - Fire down below. Fetch a bucket of water cause there's fire down below". In this song one of the participants was Audrey Porter who lived in the village. Apart from her drum which she banged, she had a car horn under her foot which she continually pressed to imitate the fire engine.

Christmas time was great fun. All the children brought ingredients for the big Christmas pudding which was mixed in a large bowl, each of us having a stir. The pudding was then taken over to Mrs. Jenning's house, "Blue Lyons" in Widford Road. She cooked it ready for the Christmas party when sweets and other goodies were bought from Dorking, the village shop.

A sad occasion occurred on 8th December 1938. All the school had a stir of the Christmas pudding when Miss Rankin the Headmistress came into the classroom to tell us that one of our friends, Betty Day had run into the road opposite her house next to the church and had been knocked down by a car and killed. We were all very sorry as Betty was a lovely girl. She came from a large family living with her parents and many brothers and sisters in farm cottages at the back of the church. Her dad was a Cowman at nearby Hodges Widford Hall Farm. She was buried in the churchyard right close to her school classroom.

Next door to Mr. Jenning's house was a tennis court. Mr. Jenning's ran a business in his yard as an Artesian Well Engineer, employing a number of village men. Long since gone, but adjacent to Mr. Jenning's tennis court, was the village blacksmith's shop. Before the second world war, this was a going concern and many a day have I spent watching the smithy at work. I think his name was Mr. Hammond who lived in a house further down the road beyond the railway bridge. There is a song called "Underneath the spreading Chestnut Tree, there the village smithy said he loved me". Well our smithy did have his premises underneath a beautiful Chestnut Tree.

Dorking was the village shop. Ma and Pa Dorking ran this. They were quite old before the war. Pa Dorking always wore a shirt without a collar and served in the shop in his slippers. Ma was a lady who always wore an apron and had her hair piled on top with a bun. The shop sold everything and also acted as a Post Office.

During the war when rationing was on, my parents used to send me in to the shop to get cigarettes for them.

Though my parents were regular customers, it was always hard work getting any from Ma and Pa Dorking even though the previous customer had bought some. They seemed to think they were the only people who could smoke or issue cigarettes. They lost a lot of customers because of their attitude.

I sang in the church choir for many years. First the Reverend Thurlow was the Vicar and later on Canon Herbert Leslie Pike who came to Widford from Newfoundland with his wife Enid, Lottie their housemaid and Llewelyn Colley, his best friend who was a lay reader at the church.

SAINT MARY'S CHURCH,

WIDFORD.    371

Fred Spalding
Photo
Chelmsford

copyright

"Daddy" Gardiner a schoolmaster was the organist and choirmaster. His wife, two sons and daughter were also members of the choir. Practise was on Wednesday evenings. We attended 11 a.m. and 6.30 p.m. services and once a month the 8 a.m. service. In addition I had to attend Sunday school at 2.30 p.m. with Mr. Albert Gooch the Sunday school teacher plus weddings and funerals as required. For all of this I got 3/6d per term plus extras for funerals and weddings.

My father and two uncles, John and Lionel were Sidesmen and my brother Michael was in the choir. He sang a number of solos. I only sang a few. Choir boys I remember were Nigel and Ian Gardiner, Kenneth, Derek, Roy and Brian Meadowcroft, Gordon "Pussy" Harris, Bob Harris, Geoffrey and Peter Moore, Robert and Brian Barden, David Bell and Norman Skingley.

The men were Alec Bewers, Tom Jarvis, Gus Owers, Arthur Turner and Harry Fisher. The ladies, Mrs. Gardiner, Miss Munday, Miss Veil and Miss Kitty Fisher. Sometimes a Mrs. Harknett joined them.

Widford had a good set of bells which were rung regularly by a team of bell ringers, mainly from other churches as not enough local people were available. They also had a set of chimes in the choir vestry on which I rang simple hymns each Sunday morning and evening. These are no longer in operation.

After services, together with a number of the choir boys, I went regularly during the various seasons bird-nesting, snowballing, swimming, or playing football and cricket.

I joined the Widford Cubs who used the Scout hut at the rear of Widford school; later on I joined the Scouts. Our Cub mistress was Mrs. Treloar who lived in Wood Street. Her husband Sandy was the Scout Master. I was Patrol Leader of Rattlesnake and later on was Assistant Troop Leader to Les Bell. However sport was a greater attraction for me and I left the troop rather early.

Easter was always a time to remember. The services were rather sombre but we always sang Stainer's Crucifixion and after the Good Friday services, we went to a lantern show in the Village Hall where Canon Pike related the Passion Story and the Crucifixion of Christ.

The village gardening and allotment show was an annual attraction in July when the men and women of the village competed against each other for the various trophies. As children we had special classes, one of which was to catch the most white butterflies which were a menace during wartime to the home grown green vegetables. My brother and I nearly always won this class.

The Vicarage near to the church housed the annual garden party hosted by the vicar. Many side-shows took place and my favourite was to throw tennis balls to try and knock the topper of the man walking backwards and forwards behind a net. I enjoyed this, particularly when it was my father behind the net. I was a crack shot and many times removed his topper.

During the war, the place known now as Widford Prep School, was run by Mr. Henry Witham Senior as the Head of the ARP in this area. My father was first in the Home Guard at County Hall where he worked and later as an ARP Warden and fire watcher. We as a family were very concerned as there was a petrol distribution centre at the corner of Wood Street. We thought if this was hit by a bomb, it might spread to our house.

My father saw an incendiary bomb drop in the petrol station and it was only by his quick action that this was put out before any damage was done.

My parents not only had my grandparents staying with them for some part of the war, but during the evenings, Mrs. Cissie Rowe, wife of Sid Rowe from the Fish and Chip shop in Springfield Road, stayed with her. She was really scared of being alone with the bombs dropping. Her husband collected her in the late evening to take her to her home in Wood Street.

I remember on one particularly bad evening with bombs dropping around the town, my mother was very worried that my grandfather was out. In those days I was not told where he was but apparently every evening he went to the Rising Sun in London Road for his pint of stout. My dad had to go down to the pub and haul him out. Neither of them were very pleased about this.

Opposite our house and near the roundabout, was a large field, now covered in houses. A barrage balloon was erected here and the airman looking after it came over to our house regularly for a bath and refreshment. One day Ted, an airman came in with a big bag of mushrooms he had collected from the field. We had a wonderful fry up but next day we were very ill as some of the mushrooms must have been toadstools.

Childhood memories bring back my stay in hospital with Scarlatina. I was carted off following a bathe in the River Wid. I caught a fish hook in my thumb and this turned poisonous and eventually led to illness. I went to the Baddow Road Isolation Hospital and was in there for six weeks. It was horrible under the watchful eye of Sister Epps.

The boys of the village often came to our house to borrow my football as it was impossible during the war to obtain replacement rubber bladders. My father, who was also a well known football referee, agreed that the boys could borrow the ball providing I was allowed in their team.

Like all young boys we had our mischievous moments. Scrumping, bird nesting and playing tricks on neighbours was part of the daily activity. No television existed and the wireless was never listened to by young boys. We made our own entertainment with hoops, conkers, tops, marbles, cigarette card throwing and roller skating in addition to five stones, a game of real skill.

The local bobby who kept an eye on us was P.C. Larrett (behind his back he was called "Larry" and sometimes "Goaty") the latter because he kept a number of goats in the field adjacent to his house. He was a genial copper and if I remember was called a Special Constable - in other words, a part-time policeman. He however was regarded by us as a man of the law and had to be respected, but we always tried to keep one step ahead of him.

Sometimes we would organise a scrumping expedition to Major Wilks garden in the old Widford Road. Several of us would climb over the wall at the back whilst one always kept watch. Little did we know that Larry had been keeping an eye of us and came round the front way to catch us red-handed. We all got told off and a short clip round the ears with a threat that he would tell our dads. He never did, and as I grew older I felt that he might have gone scrumping himself as a boy. He did not have any sons to chastise but three daughters Mary, Jean and Ruth. The latter was my age and we went to the same school.

"Larry" also asked for all the kitchen scraps to be taken to his house for the goats and chickens. Sometimes he gave us some eggs or apples. The house where the family lived was pulled down in 1994 and now a very imposing residence is there with magnificent views to Hylands Park and the River Wid.

Painting with water colours was a pastime of many of the boys in the village. "Hikey" Reg Baldwin used to sit in the River Wid with an easel near the white bridge along the London Road and paint water colours of rushes, herons and other birds. He was a good water colour artist. I painted other scenes including Widford Church. I sold this painting to Canon Pike who had it in his study for many years.

Chapter Twenty One

# REFLECTIONS

The happenings and events mentioned in the previous chapters are a true reflection of life over 50 years ago in the mid to late 1940's. At that time, in comparison to today 2002, habits and customs have changed and it is worth recording some of these in this chapter.

The milkman used to have a horse and cart and issued milk to the housewife from a large churn. The housewife took her jug to the milkman and when she returned to the house she put a muslin cover over the top. This was weighted down with beads to prevent unwanted insects entering. No refrigerator, only what was called a "safe" for the milk and other items such as butter, cheese, bacon etc. The "safe" was made of wood with fine wire mesh on all sides. This was supposed to keep the items cool and prevent insects etc., from entering.

Cheeses were put into an odd shaped dish and presented to the table. When the family had finished their meal the cheese was returned in the dish to the "safe".

Shopping was either done by visiting the town to the local grocery stores or from the deliveryman at the door. In the latter case this was restricted shopping as the deliveryman did not have a variety of items for sale due to lack of space on his vehicle.

The shops provided the best answer to the housewife although she had to return heavily laden with her goods as there were no shopping trolleys, usually a wicker basket was the main carrying source and that in itself was sometimes a bulky and heavy item.

Sugar was sold and weighed as required and put into blue paper bags. Biscuits were often at the side of the counter in large tins and when sold were put into ordinary paper bags. Butter was taken from a large tub and made into butter "pats" by the grocer who handled the butter with two wooden items with serrated faces to make the butter "pats".

Chairs were provided for the weary housewife in the store as she waited for her requirements including the grinding of coffee beans, which again after preparation were put into paper bags. Most other items in the grocery stores were sold loose and the grocer put them into ready prepared bags.

Door to door vendors often called on the housewife. In addition to the grocer with his horse and cart, there was the knife grinder who took knives to be sharpened in the street. Sometimes he would have a machine on the cart and another would have a similar contraption on a bicycle. When he pedalled the bicycle in a stationary position, the knife would be sharpened in the two sandstone's fixed in the position where a carrying basket would normally be.

Other daily or weekly visitors was the paraffin delivery man for the oil lamps or heating the stoves, the vegetable man with a large amount of fresh fruit and vegetables, the coalman with his heavy sacks of coal or coke brought to the street on a horse and cart. The rag and bone man who collected any old clothes you had available. If you were lucky, you got a tanner for a rabbit skin.

In those days families lived to a certain extent off the land with rabbits, hares, ducks, pheasants and pigeons supplementing the weekly meat requirements.

On the odd occasion, gypsies would knock at your door selling clothes pegs and the odd piece of heather or lavender. Tramps would ask if you could fill their billycans with water and, did you have the odd piece of bread?

Buses were the main means of transport for people living in outlying districts and bicycles for those travelling to work in the shops and factories. You could leave your bike adjacent to the pavement or against a wall and it would still be there when you returned even after a day or so.

Money at that time was in £'s shillings and pence, measurements in yards, feet and inches, and weights in tons, hundredweights and pounds.

Television was not available to many homes, only the wireless or, to give it the modern term the radio. Families made their own amusement mainly singing or piano playing or some other form of musical entertainment. Many of the best songs were written in those days and because of the words, are well remembered even today.

Various games were played by the children many of which are not heard of today. There were hoops, a large 3 or 4 foot diameter circle of either wood or steel which was pushed with a stick up and down the street, marbles with small glass balls or large alleys as they were called. Five stones, this was an interesting game played with five small blocks of hardened clay and the idea was to carry out as many decreed functions as possible before passing the stones to the next person. Cigarette cards, skating them up against a wall to cover one and win all those present or to knock one down and again win all. Skating on the pavements or in the playground. Tops, beating a wooden top with a stick which had a piece of leather or string attached.

In the summer, especially when the weather was hot, the familiar sound of the ice cream man ringing his handbell or bicycle bell was a welcome sound for the younger generation. The "Walls" ice cream was a particular favourite. The man on his three wheeler bicycle and the large refrigerated box in front offered a wide choice of plain, chocolate or flavoured ice creams. The favourite was a three cornered fruit flavoured lolly which went down with most children and at 3d was very cheap.

Families made their own enjoyments. The cinema and the dance halls were the favourite places to visit especially at weekends. Chelmsford had four main cinemas the "Ritz" later renamed the "Odeon", the "Regent" which acted as a theatre for some events, the "Pavilion" in Rainsford Road and the "Select" in New Writtle Street. The latter had a bad name and was often referred to as the "Fleapit". Saturday mornings at the "Ritz" was the best place to go for the young boys and girls. The main film was always Flash Gordon and the supplementaries Mickey Mouse or something with Shirley Temple as the star.

Families went out for walks at the weekends to explore the countryside, especially in the summer months. They took picnics to eat at their various destinations. Bicycles were prevalent for longer trips and also for people travelling to and from their workplace although buses at lunch times often conveyed them to their homes and back again after a one hour lunch break.

If you did not have a garden then you rented an allotment. This was carrying on a wartime tradition as the slogan in the 1939-45 war was "back to the land" and "dig for victory". My parents had an allotment firstly near the canal in Navigation Road when we lived in Hill Road and later on, the corner of Wood Street when we moved to Widford. Most villagers competed in the annual garden and allotment show, usually held in July each year. I remember on one occasion together with my younger brother we won a prize for collecting the most number of white butterflies and putting them in a picture frame. Apparently these were an enemy of the gardener and he was delighted to get rid of them before they laid their eggs.

The countryside had plenty to offer in the way of wild fruit and at the appropriate time of the year we would go out and collect mushrooms, blackberries, chestnuts, walnuts, sloes, crab apples and even watercress. These were brought to the home and prepared and either eaten or bottled for use at a later time.

Homemade jams and pickles were great favourites and again the various requirements for these were gathered at the appropriate time and prepared for winter storage. The smell of oranges being prepared on the cooker for marmalade brings back happy memories of those bygone days.

In the countryside, many wild flowers grew. At Easter time and on Mothers day, the children went into the woods and fields to collect these and bring them to their mothers. The hedgerows were much taller in those days and protected the various species from the savage winter winds and frost.

In winter the obvious delight of young boys was the snowfall and the building of snowmen and snowball fights with others. When a very hard frost was prevalent the ponds froze and ice skating on them was another past time.

Chelmsford had a low population in comparison to the present day. Around 35,000 until it became a commuter town with the boundaries extended and the population increased to something as it is today of 150,000. Some of the roads in the area were just dirt tracks. Those which come to mind were Longstomps Avenue and Waterhouse Lane. There were no houses or factories, just fields round these areas and very few vehicles. It was well after the last war before these two roads were made up and with that, the houses and traffic flow increased in leaps and bounds.

Chelmsford town centre had very little mechanised transport flowing through the centre. Mainly omnibuses and transport lorries. Even the High Street and Duke Street had vehicular traffic going in both directions. The only time when the place got crowded was at lunch times and leaving off time for the factories.

Market day in Chelmsford was a real event with animals being driven from the Railway Goods Yard in New Street to the Cattle Market in appropriately named Market Road. Many a time animals escaped and had to be chased by the drovers to get them back to their destination. Even the cattle when purchased were driven on the public highway until they reached the farm where they were to find their next home.

The third Friday of the month was always destined as a horse sale day and the gypsies made a special effort to attend bringing with them to the sale ring horses which they owned. They used to congregate behind the Golden Fleece in Duke Street and drink themselves silly. Often a fight would break out and the local bobby was called to quieten things down. One day a husband and wife had a row and she threw her wedding ring at her husband. He could not find it. Some two days later I saw this shiny ring at the side of the road and took it to the local police station. It was never claimed and my mother took charge of this for her own jewellery box.

The biggest department store was that owned by Messrs J. and G. Bond. They had three stores, one in Duke Street, one in High Street and one in Moulsham Street. They were often referred to as top, middle and bottom Bonds.

Rankins in Moulsham Street was a favourite place to buy any amount of clothes for children and adults. The delivery boy who rode a large trade bicycle is one of my characters in a previous chapter. He was Jones.

During winter, home pastimes were mainly the wireless and games plus of course playing instruments. The wireless particularly for children provided a lot of entertainment. Uncle Mac was a real favourite for "Children's Hour" as was Larry the Lamb and Mr. Grouser.

"In Town Tonight" brought together at the weekends, people who were in London at that time. "Monday Night at Eight o'clock Oh Can't You Hear the Chimes", was a real favourite for both adults and children alike.

Politeness, a thing which is missing today with many people both young and old was very prevalent after the 1939-45 war. Gentlemen and young people holding doors open for others rather than let them slam in your face as is often the case today. Gentlemen and boys raising their hat or caps to a lady or an elder was very important and strictly adhered to. Most boys and men in those days wore a cap or hat.

Various ethics were also in force, particularly at meal times where it was said that the most important thing was to eat your food and not talk. There were louts about but never like today where wanton destruction of items in parks and thefts from shops and houses regularly take place. You could leave your house door open or unlocked without fear that somebody would break or come in. Children in prams were left outside shops knowing they would still be there when the parent returned. The same was with bicycles. They could be left outside a shop or house. I knew somebody who left his bike outside a shop against the kerb for over a week. He could not remember where he had left it until passing by later he saw the bike exactly in the place where he had left it.

Coal and coke fires were much in evidence and in winter these caused a lot of smog. We were not cosseted like today with central heating. If you wanted toast for your tea or breakfast you put a slice of bread on a toasting fork and held it over the hot burning coal or coke fire.

People had time to go to church regularly on a Sunday and most children attended Sunday school in the afternoon. Some boys were even in the local choir attending church on three occasions on a Sunday plus Sunday school

Christmas time was great fun. No television, you made your own entertainment with many party games such as charades, postman's knock and pinning the tail on the Donkey whilst being blindfolded. The children made the paper chains for decorating the house and filled the crackers with small presents. Mother made the Christmas Puddings and the Cake and the children always had a stir of the ingredients before they were cooked or baked. In those days silver three-penny pieces were put into the Christmas Puddings and it was a delight of young children that they found one usually after being told to eat the Pudding first.

Smells of various kinds were more noticeable in those days. The gasworks in Navigation Road, the tannery behind the "Ritz" Cinema, coal and coke burning on the fires. The rag and bone merchants place in Baddow Road where the rabbit skins were hung outside to dry. The coffee grinding machine in Duke Street, the smell of dung from the horses as they traversed the town pulling either the coal or milk carts.

These are but a few reflections of life some fifty years ago. The pace of life was much slower than today. People had time to talk to each other, were more friendly and polite and involved themselves in pioneering events and setting up good causes.